# PREACHING
# WITH
Connecting with
Postmodern Listeners
# CONVICTION

## Kenton C. Anderson

kregel
PUBLICATIONS

Grand Rapids, MI  49

*Preaching with Conviction: Connecting with Postmodern Listeners*

© 2001 by Kenton C. Anderson

Published by Kregel Publications, a division of Kregel, Inc., P.O. Box 2607, Grand Rapids, MI 49501. Kregel Publications provides trusted, biblical publications for Christian growth and service. Your comments and suggestions are valued. For more information about Kregel Publications, visit our web site: www.kregel.com.

ISBN 0-8254-2020-2

Printed in the United States of America

1 2 3 4 5 / 05 04 03 02 01

To my gracious listeners—
especially Karen

# Contents

# Foreword

Ours is an age of suspicion. We are suspicious of government, of business, of our neighbors. We question authority at all levels, and God does not escape this cynicism that envelops the postmodern mind.

That reality has profound implications for preaching. How do you proclaim God's truth in an age when the entire culture seems to be based on moral and philosophical relativism? Is it possible to preach with authority and conviction in such a context?

Kent Anderson believes it is, and this book provides a guide to that process. Using a narrative approach with a fictional preacher as the main character, Kent voices the same questions all preachers ask themselves in an age of doubt. *Preaching with Conviction* walks the reader through the purpose and place of preaching in a postmodern era, and reveals both hope and insight for the future of preaching.

The book is less a travel guide than a shared journey that allows us to see through the eyes of a fellow struggler who seeks to communicate God's truth in a challenging time and place. Any reader who has stood in the pulpit to preach will relate to the pastor in this story: the questions he asks himself, the challenges he encounters, and the power from above that ultimately makes the difference.

In a culture of questions, the gospel provides answers. For those of us who seek to communicate that truth effectively, this book offers a word of encouragement and insight.

—MICHAEL DUDUIT
Editor, *Preaching* magazine

# Preface

I haven't actually used a pulpit in several years. Long ago, I discovered that I didn't need a place to rest my notes and, thus, the pulpit began to feel extraneous. I wondered whether the furniture might actually be getting in the way, creating an unnecessary barrier between my listeners and me. Eventually I found the courage to move out from behind the comforting protection of the pulpit in an attempt to speak more directly to the people. I did feel a little vulnerable out there, but the congregation seemed to like it. Today, listeners tell me that they appreciate it when I look them in the eye and get out in front of them without the barrier that the pulpit presents.

This is one signal of a significant shift in people's attitudes regarding the preaching task. I cannot imagine hearing my childhood pastor preach without a pulpit. He mounted the platform of our church and stood behind that familiar wooden desk every Sunday for forty-two years. Without the pulpit, he would have seemed naked. The pulpit was the place of preaching. It was the furniture of authority.

Recently, however, preachers have sensed the need to shake things up, experimenting with new models and alternative approaches. Postmodern thinking is less willing to invest authority in a piece of furniture. In fact, the postmodern mind would question the value of the homiletic task altogether. To *pro-claim* anything in these days of subjective underconfidence would seem audacious. Preachers who want to speak powerfully will need to offer something more authoritative than a pulpit.

The following manuscript describes my justification for preaching in postmodern times. It also modestly suggests how we might pursue the task. The book has grown out of the Ph.D. dissertation I wrote at Southwestern Baptist Theological Seminary in 1996, "'Global' Preaching: A Paradigm for Preaching Across Cultural Change." Of course, in keeping with the spirit of postmodernism, the form of presentation for this work has changed dramatically.

The light mystery form of this manuscript integrates several elements that transcend the fictional elements of the story. The sermon Jack Newman prepares and preaches is an actual sermon I preached at Parkland Fellowship Church, Surrey, B.C., in August of 2000. You can hear this sermon as it was originally preached in streaming audio by logging on to my Web site, www.preaching.org (yes, it is a real Web site). The article that Jack reads off the Web actually exists, too. It is also available on the site and is reprinted as an appendix to this book.

Throughout the book, the reader will find various charts and other information designed to add to the reading experience and lend a certain scholarly flavor to the book. The novel form is not intended to diminish the academic value of the work. Of course, inclusion of comments does not mean the author endorses everything said. Many of the quotations are there for the purpose of stimulation and provocation. The reader is encouraged to sift and sort.

The mystery novel form provides more than just interest. It allows the reader to consider the mysteriousness of the gospel and of the preaching task itself. It also models, to some degree, the integration of narrative and exposition that the book counsels.

That God still speaks through human mouthpieces is one of the best things I know. This book is offered in the hope that many more "Jack Newmans" can rediscover the joy of preaching in these postmodern times.

# 1

# The Postmodern Problem

The pulpit mocked him. Rooted and immovable like an old-growth Douglas fir, it stood its defiant ground. Hand-built by some forgotten craftsman, this pulpit had served many a preacher. The shouters and the shriekers, the pounders and the pleaders, had all found shelter and a certain authority behind its imposing bulk. Its topside edges, oiled and smoothed by the uncalloused hands of countless preachers, bore witness to its durability. "I was here before you, and I'll be here long after you are gone," it taunted.

The arrogant pulpit intimidated its present occupant. The Reverend Jackson Newman was feeling the pressure. Sensing the ghosts of preachers past, he felt small and transparent whenever he took his place behind this "sacred desk." He couldn't find the expected punch. The authority necessary for dynamic preaching had long since escaped him. His sermons were no match for this tradition-steeped pulpit. It was only a matter of time.

The glass broke with a dull crack, muted by a wadded-up towel. There was no alarm to worry about at the offices of the Green Valley Trust. No one had ever considered the possibility of a break-in, given the dated computers and meager resources housed on the premises. Green Valley was a small, but vocal, environmental protection lobby, which, of course, meant little to the young men who forced entry.

The building was dark and broken down. It was the kind of place you would expect to find a shoestring charity with more mission than money. You could trace the history of the building by the several strata of paint colors in evidence where the exterior was particularly worn. It had been a food market (painted blue), a clothing store (sensible white), a military recruiting office (army green), a coffeehouse run by the youth group from the church half a block away (creamy yellow), and a campaign office for several failed local candidates (red, white, and blue). The current occupants hadn't bothered with a fresh coat of paint. It's hard to justify a painting contractor when you're trying to save the rain forest.

The second of the two young men crawled carefully, head first, through the window, trying not to leave fingerprints on the glass. His partner was already inside. It was uncomfortable trying to squeeze through the old-style wooden window opening. He supported himself by putting his hands out in front on the floor and wiggling his way in. The carpet was grimy and worn. His left hand found his partner's flip phone buried in the shag.

"Your phone fell out of your pocket," he said.

"Shut up," the other muttered. "Not so loud."

"As if anyone is going to hear us around here. The only building with any lights on is that church down the road, and ain't none of them going to be walking down this part of the street this time of night."

"Just shut up, I said."

"Tell me again why I'm here?" the second intruder asked.

"To keep me company," said the first, his tone of voice securing the silence he demanded.

When did this happen? wondered the second young man. He could hear the voice of his mother somewhere in the back of his head. She had often warned him about the company he kept. Maybe he should have listened more carefully. When did he graduate to breaking-and-entering, like some character in a bad police drama? He imagined himself in a lineup at the precinct—an uncomfortable thought. What were you supposed to do in a lineup anyway? Look unconcerned? Smile even? What if they thought you were trying to hide something! "Number three, step forward," they'd say. "And wipe that stupid smile off your face."

The room was cluttered with paper, newspapers, computer printouts, press releases—nothing of much interest. A glow-in-the-dark clock cast an eerie light over the proceedings.

"I think I found something," said the first man.

"Good. Can we get out of here now?" replied the second.

"Not until we've trashed the place a little," grunted the first.

"Why do you want to do that? Let's just get out of here while we can."

"Just do it. C'mon, throw some stuff around." The first had already started, pulling out drawers and scattering papers. His partner half-heartedly knocked over a pot of cold coffee. The liquid spread rapidly across the desktop staining a stack of file folders.

At last the first man seemed satisfied. "Okay, let's go out the back. We can cut through the alley."

The cold night air was a slap in the face. The moonlight cast the alley in contrasting patches of brightness and dark. Cautiously, the two quick-walked their way from building to building. They paused in a sheltered spot, under a stairwell behind the neighborhood church. The first man took some papers out of a bag and stuffed them in his pocket. He let the bag fall to the ground.

"Any money?" asked the second man.

"A little," was the reply.

—·<ᴄᴄᴄ·ᴘ·ᴅᴅᴅᴅ>·—

Jackson Newman sat quietly in his office. It was an unusual place for a study, built as it was above the sanctuary on the back end of the church, three stories up from the alleyway. There had probably been a decent view from this elevated position seventy-five years earlier when the building had been constructed, but it was long since obstructed by a warehouse. The warehouse used to house furniture; now it was empty.

The pastor thought he heard voices from the alley. Kind of late for that, he thought. But then look at me, he reminded himself. It's not too late for me to be here this time of night, obsessing about my sermon. He looked out the window just long enough to see two young men, but he didn't give it much thought. Probably up to no good, he told himself. The pastor had long ago given up on the neighborhood.

It was just another late Sunday night, and Pastor Jack was tired. How long had he been doing this now? he wondered. Twenty years? Twenty-two? How many sermons would that have been? Too many, he decided. Maybe it was just midlife. Maybe if he could get some exercise; he'd put on a few pounds the last couple of years. His dark brown hair was showing a little more gray than it used to. His blue eyes had lost some of their sparkle.

Jack found himself focused on the bottom left-hand drawer of his beaten desk. With a tug and a slight twist to the left, he opened it. Reaching in, he took out a letter and fingered it thoughtfully.

"Dear brothers and sisters, it is with great regret and prayerful consideration . . ."

He remembered his old homiletics professor from seminary days saying that a pastor should never resign on Sunday night. Well, he had written the letter, but he hadn't sent it to the board members . . . at least not yet.

———

*The Church needs to know what the world wants to hear, and yet also find a way to give what it needs to hear in a sermon.*

CALVIN MILLER, *MARKETPLACE PREACHING*, 31.

It was so much simpler in those days. He'd looked forward to his career as a pastor. It had seemed like such an honorable thing to do. He dreamed of making a difference—of changing the world through his preaching. He'd thought people would respect him. The position itself had carried authority back then. But no longer. Now, preaching had become a kind of adversarial challenge. "Prove to me that what you're saying is worth the investment of my time," the people seemed to say. "Show me why I should care. Grab me. . . . Entertain me. . . ."

He could see it in their faces. And it wasn't just the regular hard-boiled types. It was the whole congregation. The mother whose daughter didn't arrive home until three in the morning—he could see it in the droop in her eyes. The man with football tickets in his pocket. If the sermon was over quickly enough, and he could hit the traffic just right, he might be able to get into his seat before kickoff. "Three Truths of the Trinity" doesn't have much chance against the Packers–Cowboys or a mother's tired anxiety.

The Reverend Jackson Newman, M.Div., stood up deliberately, gathered his notes from the morning's sermon, and dropped them reverently into the garbage. He glanced at the notes he'd begun for the following Sunday's sermon. Impulsively, he trashed them, too. The letter, however, he carefully returned to the bottom left drawer. He would leave it there—for now.

He felt a little empty as he left the office to go home. At least offerings were up, he reminded himself. Things weren't all bad. Not yet, at least. He had to go out the back way in order not to trip the alarm. There was some garbage in the alley by the stairs. Probably those prowlers, he thought.

—⋘⋙—

Thomas Newman was at his desk when the phone rang. A break-in wouldn't normally warrant the attention of a journalist of Newman's experience, but someone thought this one might have political implications, so it had been tossed in his direction. He checked his notes before calling the camera crew and jumping in his car.

Dogwood Developments had won approval with a narrow vote by

city council to build a golf course and high-end housing project on a sensitive piece of land on the city's south end. The mayor's promise to remove the property from the agricultural land reserve had provoked a sharp response from Stephen Lang of the Green Valley Trust. Lang had a long history of fierce opposition to Dogwood's attempts to develop sensitive properties around the city. Harsh words had ensued— threats even, if rumors could be believed.

Now, the offices at Green Valley had been vandalized and documents stolen. Not that he believed the mayor's office was involved. Anybody could have broken into the building, especially in that part of town. Nevertheless, the situation was sure to be politically charged.

"Terri, call city hall for some kind of comment on this, could you? Councilman Andrews has been blowing a lot of steam lately." Setting down his cell phone, he remembered to call his brother. They had agreed to have lunch.

—⟨⟨⟨⟨⟨⟩⟩⟩⟩⟩—

The restaurant was past its glory, but it maintained a certain charm. The place had been the venue for Newman family birthdays and anniversaries for several decades. It was run-down now, like the neighborhood that surrounded it. The authentic Chinese ambiance was gone, the buffet replaced by a traditional western menu, and the immigrant Chinese waitresses had been replaced by students of various ethnic origins. Despite the changes, the food was passable and the brothers enjoyed the anonymity of the place.

"Is this the Right Reverend Newman I'm dining with?" Tom teased. "If you're in disguise, it's perfect!"

Jack was wearing sweatpants redeemed from the dirty clothes hamper. Chin stubble was sprouting. He wasn't ready to respond to his well-meaning brother. He wanted to nurse his misery before giving voice to it.

"Any openings at the station?" he finally asked. "How 'bout the weather. I'd make a great weatherman, I think."

"Meteorologist, you mean. Nowadays, you have to have a college degree to do the weather. Besides, you've got a job, Jack. What are you talking about?"

"Yeah. A weatherman," Jack ignored his brother. "Nobody worries about it when the weatherman gets it wrong. He just gives his report, and everybody understands it has nothing to do with reality. Nobody gets mad at the weatherman. I could be a good weath—"

"That bad, huh?"

"Tom, I don't even want to tell people what I do for a living anymore. I'm a preacher. A *preacher*, for goodness sake! That's virtually an expletive in our culture. If you really want to get under a person's skin, what do you say? 'Don't *preach* at me!' As if preaching was the most offensive thing a person could do."

"It's true," Tom offered. "One of my colleagues just did a piece on the leader of the Alternative Party the other day. Called him impatient, intolerant, and arrogant. You know what his tag line was? Said he was a *preacher* not a politician."

---

*But it is no longer tenable for us to assert our beliefs about Jesus—about divinity, about resurrection, about his being the only path to God—as final, complete, and unalterable for every human being everywhere. This is a deeply disturbing notion, to say the least, particularly for preachers, whose very livelihoods have depended upon those precise affirmations.*

JOSEPH M. WEBB, "PLURALISM AND THE
SEARCH FOR A 'NEW GOSPEL,'" 56.

"I saw that," Jack replied. "But do you know the worst part? I'm starting to agree with them. I mean, here we are living in a pluralistic world with hundreds of different cultures and subcultures all around us. Everybody has a point of view and everybody has a right to it. Then here comes the preacher, claiming to know the truth for all time, claiming to speak for God, claiming to know what's best for everyone else. I mean, really! Is there anything more arrogant than a preacher?"

"Trash-talking point guards?" Tom suggested helpfully. "Banana republic despots? I could tell you about a few of them I've interviewed."

"I'm serious," Jack complained.

"Look, Jack," Tom said, "you know I've never really supported your career in the first place. I've never bought into the whole 'faith thing' like you have. But you shouldn't be so hard on yourself. Sure, times have changed, and things are different. But good grief, we're always going to have preachers. And you're a good one, Jack. I mean, look at you. You actually care about this stuff!"

---

*The postmodern consciousness has abandoned the Enlightenment belief in inevitable progress. Postmoderns have not sustained the optimism that characterized the previous generations. To the contrary, they evidence a gnawing pessimism. For the first time in recent history, the emerging generation does not share the conviction of their parents that the world is becoming a better place in which to live. From widening holes in the ozone layer to teen on teen violence, they see our problems mounting. And they are no longer convinced that human ingenuity will solve these enormous problems or that their living standard will be higher than that of their parents.*

STANLEY J. GRENZ, *A PRIMER ON POSTMODERNISM*, 13.

"I used to be good," countered Jack, "at least, I thought I was. But things have really changed. The world isn't what it used to be."

"That's true enough," Tom said.

"They've got a word for it, you know—*postmodernity*."

"I've seen that, but I've got no idea what it means."

"It's not that complicated, really," Jack said. "As best I can tell, from the reading I've done, when you boil it down to its essence, post–modernism is a confidence thing."

"What do you mean?" asked Tom.

"Do you remember the movie *Titanic*?" Jack asked.

"Of course," said Tom.

"You've got this great unsinkable ship, this marvelous piece of high technology, a symbol of man's ability to rise above the limitations of nature and conquer his world."

"Except it sunk," Tom observed.

"It sunk," Jack affirmed, "and with it our self-confidence sunk a little bit, too. Sure, we would still put a man on the moon, and we'd figure out how to build a microchip—but it just seems that the more we achieve, the less confident we are. The more we know, the more we know we'll never know."

"I know," Tom smiled.

"You know *nothing*," Jack declared, "and that's the problem. Never before have people been so aware of their limits."

Tom wiped his fingers on the napkin. The spring rolls were a little greasy today.

### The Postmodern Problem

- ▶ Mystery
- ▶ Plurality
- ▶ Technology

"We used to count on science," Jack said. "But even the scientists these days are caught up in the mystery. We build powerful microscopes to observe the mysteries of subatomic particles. We built the Hubble telescope to plumb the farthest reaches. We're looking for answers to our questions. Yet, for every question we answer we discover ten or twenty more that we didn't even know existed. Quantum mechanics, Heisenberg's uncertainty principle. Even the scientists are telling us there's a fundamental mystery at the very core of our lives. The more we study this stuff, the more painfully aware we become of just how little we actually know about any of it."

Tom looked Jack over more carefully than normal. "I didn't know you thought so much about this."

"There's more," Jack said. "Not only is it a question of mystery, but it's also a matter of plurality."

"The 'Global Village,'" Tom replied.

"Exactly," said Jack. "We've got more cultures and worldviews represented in the four blocks surrounding this restaurant than we used to see in the whole country a few decades ago."

"What's wrong with that?" Tom answered defensively.

"Nothing at all," Jack said. "I love the diversity—except that it increases the complexity of our lives. There's no consensus about what to believe anymore, because as soon as we assert a point someone else comes along to knock it down and tear it apart or at least to raise a healthy dose of reasonable doubt. We don't want to offend people of different beliefs by making strong religious statements. The guy two blocks down and a half block over might be a Buddhist. Who's to say, really, whether he's right or wrong." Jack looked around the restaurant. "Look at that guy over there." As if to emphasize his point, a man with a turban on his head sat two tables over, eating a hamburger—and they were all in a Chinese restaurant. "He's got a right to his view, doesn't he? Whatever it is, he might even be correct."

"My problem," Tom said, "is technology. It's just about killing me in my business. On the one hand, you've got more information available than ever before. On the other, you've got less time to respond. Technology like e-mail and faxes has greatly increased the speed of public discourse. Used to be you could defer problems by sending a letter. It'd take two weeks before you had to do anything about it. Now the letter's gone, and you've got a response back in seconds. You've got to run a whole lot faster."

"Technology overwhelms people," Jack said. "With the Internet, CD-ROM, and whatever is coming next, people have more access to information than we ever imagined. But, instead of empowering people, all this information leaves them feeling like they're falling behind."

"It's a mixed blessing," Tom agreed. "A hundred years ago it took half a century or more for the world to double its knowledge base. Now it happens every other year. A person used to have time to deal with this information, but now staying current is a nightmare."

"Too much information, too fast, means life is too unpredictable," Jack mused. "There are too many factors beyond our control. Our problem is that we don't know what we don't know. As a result, we're unable to forecast the future, and that leaves us feeling vulnerable. It's virtually impossible to maintain a sense of confidence about yourself when you've lost the handles on life. As a result, people today have a well-developed sense of tentativeness. They're afraid to make commitments, because they know they could never have all the facts."

"That makes for a very difficult preaching environment," Tom suggested.

"No kidding!" Jack agreed. "Many of the preachers I know have given up trying to keep up. They've lost confidence, and it shows in their preaching!"

"So this is what people mean when I hear them talking about postmodernism?"

"Yeah," Jack said, "but it's a little deeper than that. It's more philosophical. Postmodernism is shorthand for three very difficult questions, and all of them are about truth."

"What are they?"

"Okay, the first is, 'Does truth exist?'"

"The age-old conundrum," Tom said. "What's the second?"

"'Can truth be known?'" Jack answered.

"And the third?"

"'Can truth be told?'"

## Key Questions

► Does truth exist?
► Can truth be known?
► Can truth be told?

"Where do you get this stuff?" Tom laughed. "When did you become Joe Philosophy?"

"I took a continuing education course last spring," Jack answered. "It was exciting at first. The prof was laying all this out for us, and I was into it because everything he was saying rang true with what I'd been experiencing. It's just that in the end, he didn't tell me what I could do about it."

"That's not much good," Tom said.

"No, but at least I know what's wrong."

There was something playing indiscernibly on the restaurant stereo. The brothers paused to eat. The chow mein was mushy; the chop suey too firm.

Tom spoke first. "So how about it?" he asked. "Does truth exist?"

"Obviously, I think so," Jack answered. "If I didn't believe in truth, I certainly couldn't preach."

"But that's your problem, isn't it?" Tom said.

"Sure," said Jack. "If there's nothing out there that's bigger than us, I've got nothing to say. If God doesn't exist, then its all arrogance."

"But people haven't really given up on God," Tom said. "I'm hearing more god-talk than ever."

---

*What the truth means here is, however,* agreement *or con-sensus* as to what shall be held to be true.

G. B. MADISON, *THE HERMENEUTICS OF POSTMODERNITY*, 31.

"That's true," Jack responded, "but you don't hear much about big-"G" God or objective truth—truth once and for all. People like to talk about *their* truth and *your* truth, but no one is talking about ultimate truth. It's do-it-yourself god. God in your own image."

"It's safer that way, I imagine," Tom said.

"Sure it is," said Jack. "That way, I don't have to face the pressure of finding *the* God. I can make him out any way I want him, and I don't have to deal with the pressure of sharing him with anyone else."

"If it's a him."

"That's right, it could be an it, a force, a place, an emotion . . ."

"But that's not God," Tom said. "A least not any kind of real God."

Jack set down his fork. The chop suey was a little heavy on the celery, too. All in all, it wasn't the best meal, and he'd about had his fill. Tom, on the other hand, seemed determined to give the dishwasher as little to do as possible.

---

*Can God speak an audible word with the words of Scripture and so be known among us as transcendent presence?*

CHARLES BARTOW, *GOD'S HUMAN SPEECH*, IX.

"The God I'm interested in," Jack said, "is a real God, the one who created the world and has a purpose for its future. I'm talking about the God of the Bible, the great I AM. Frankly, any less of a god concept than that isn't worth preaching. It's just not worth the energy."

"I think people want to believe in truth," Tom offered. "It's like *The X-Files*—the truth is out there!"

"Except that it's always just one step away, isn't it? Mulder and Scully never quite put their finger on it."

"And that's your second question, isn't it," Tom said. "Can truth be known?"

"Exactly. Even if we grant objective truth, postmodern people have serious doubts as to whether they can lay their hands on it," Jack offered.

"If truth were objective, the minute we touched it we'd stain it with our fingerprints," Tom said.

"You're right," Jack said. "Our problem is we're finite and, as a preacher, I might add, we are fallen."

"Keep talking," Tom said.

"The fact that we're finite means that we can't see it all at once. As a human being, I'm locked in time and space. I can't be in two places at once. If I'm sitting in this chair, I can't sit in your chair at the same time."

"And it's a real shame, too," Tom said. "From where you're sitting you can't see that blonde I've been enjoying for the last half hour."

"That's the point I'm trying to make," Jack said. "I can't see the blonde, because my perspective doesn't include that view."

"Okay, so why is this important?" Tom wondered.

"Postmodern philosophers argue that it's impossible to talk meaningfully about truth when no one among us can see it all at once. If we're locked into our particular point of view and our particular moment in time, how can we ever expect to speak meaningfully about objective truth for all time?"

"Okay," Tom said, "I'm getting it."

"Remember the death of Princess Diana?" Jack asked.

"Sure," Tom said. "Not one of the brightest moments for my chosen profession."

"Exactly," Jack agreed. "When the crash first occurred, you guys were all over the newscasts laying the blame at the feet of the paparazzi. Those freelance photojournalists had hounded the princess to her death."

"Ah, but not so fast," Tom said. "Remember, they discovered that the driver of Diana's limousine was drunk—three times above the legal limit. One of our network guys broke the story."

"Right," Jack said. "This new *perspective* changed the whole story, didn't it. But it didn't stop there. A couple of weeks later they found flakes of paint on the Mercedes. They traced that paint to a white Fiat . . . or was it black?"

"I don't remember."

"Doesn't matter. The point is that the story changed again. Eventually people realized that the truth wasn't so easy because there wasn't anyone who had seen the whole thing and who had all the facts. The only ones who had were either dead or, in the case of the driver, incapacitated. And that's my problem, too."

"What, you're incapacitated?" Tom asked.

"Well, yeah, in a way I am," Jack answered. "How am I supposed to get up in the pulpit and tell people *the truth* when all I can really offer is my personal perspective. Postmoderns argue that there's no privileged point of view by which we can accurately claim to know the objective truth for everyone. I'm starting to think that they're right," Jack concluded sadly.

"I see the problem," Tom nodded.

"It's even worse than that when you consider the sin issue. Even if I could get past my subjectivity, I couldn't overcome my selfishness."

A busboy came by to clear the dishes. He had a ring in his nose and another on his thumb. His hair featured three distinct hues, each competing violently with the other. He could use a shave, Jack found himself thinking—although the improvement to his appearance would be marginal, he concluded.

"There was a third question," Tom said.

"Can truth be told?" Jack reminded him.

"I sure hope so," Tom offered. "If not, I'm out of a job, too."

"Well, maybe you should dust off your résumé," Jack said. "Postmodernists tell us that there's no unbiased presentation of truth. That everything we experience in life is represented, or re-presented. Everything is mediated to us through some bias or another. You should know that more than anyone."

"What are you talking about?" Tom feigned offense. "You're talking to an *objective journalist* here."

"Yeah, right," Jack said. "You have no opinions about anything, do you. You're just a blank slate, and when you get on the eleven o'clock news all we're getting is the truth, pure and simple—untainted by any of the personal perspectives of our humble news reporter."

---

*The Bible doesn't just build on human experience. It rearranges our experience. . . .*

WILLIAM WILLIMON, *PECULIAR SPEECH*, 14.

"Of course," Tom said. He was having a hard time holding a straight face. "Actually, I think there's more hypocrisy in my profession than in most. We're all out there putting our spin on the story. The thing is, how do we avoid it? I don't know what else we can do. At least you preachers are up front about your agenda."

"We're all biased," Jack said. "We see everything through a personal grid made up of the complex web of our experiences, education, and the environment in which we grew up. We can't escape it."

"So we end up saying what we want to say," Tom said.

"And seeing what we want to see," Jack added. "We were talking about the *Titanic* earlier. I read an article recently about the site where most of the *Titanic* victims are buried. It's an obscure little cemetery near Halifax in Eastern Canada. One of the tombstones there bears the name J. Dawson."

"Jack Dawson," Tom said.

"You mean Leonardo DiCaprio," Jack said. "Jack Dawson was a fictional character invented for the movie, but that hasn't stopped hundreds of teenage girls from flocking to the grave site to leave flowers, letters, and teddy bears at this man's grave."

"Confusing fact with fiction," Tom said.

"The strange thing is that the girls know it's not really the movie character's burial place, but it doesn't seem to matter to them. It gives them more pleasure to use their imagination. And they're not alone. This kind of thing happens everywhere. Who's to say what's real anymore when the virtual world of our imagination is more compelling than the physical world of our actual lives."

The blonde was making a dramatic departure. Jack and Tom paused to watch. Her young man fumbled with the tip, his romantic bewilderment interfering with his math. She passed close enough for Jack to smell a hint of Chanel. A few weeks ago, he wouldn't have noticed. He was noticing a lot of things now.

"There's more," Jack resumed. "We haven't even talked about the problem of language, yet."

---

*Language as a stable system of normatively identical forms is merely a scientific abstraction.*

MIKHAIL BAKHTIN, "MARXISM AND THE
PHILOSOPHY OF LANGUAGE," 941.

"You mean the problem of translating from one language to another?" asked Tom.

"It's deeper than that," Jack said, "more philosophical. Language is actually a very blunt instrument. It's more difficult than we think to communicate what we mean."

"That's true enough," Tom agreed.

"We assume that words are stable, readily identifiable units of thought, capable of transmitting ideas from one person to another. In fact, it's seldom that simple. Words have multiple meanings, and they're subject to a variety of interpretations."

"That's what keeps the politicians busy," Tom observed.

"Yes!" Jack agreed. "I read that Ernest Hemingway rewrote the conclusion to *Farewell to Arms* thirty-nine times. When they asked him why, he answered, 'To get the words right.'"

"That's obsessive," Tom objected.

"Sure," Jack agreed, "but Hemingway understood the difficulty of transferring an idea from one person's mind to that of another. We can never be completely sure that the other person understands what we mean or that they're interpreting things the way we intended."

"Words are slippery little things."

"Sure are," Jack said. "Wittgenstein said it was all just a complex language game. In our attempt to *communicate* reality, we end up *forming* reality according to the spin we put on the words we use."

"Spin. Like I said, it's what keeps me in business—reporting on those politicians playing their games," Tom said.

"It may be keeping you in business, but it's driving me out of business," Jack retorted. "I'm not sure I can say what I think I mean. I mean . . ."

"I know what you mean," Tom assured him.

"Are you sure?" Jack answered. "More and more I wonder whether *I* even know what I mean."

"Yeah," Tom said, "but this isn't necessarily a bad thing, Jack. Look at you. Do you know what I see sitting here in front of me? I see an honest preacher. You're finally acting like a real human being. This is the first time in a long time that I can actually relate to most of what you're saying. So you're frustrated. You struggle with the nature of truth. Welcome to the human race! We've been waiting for you."

"Go ahead and laugh. You don't have to stand in that pulpit every week!" Jack paused to consider his coffee. He sipped it cautiously, as if he suspected it of something.

"Just tell them what you really think," Tom advised.

"Yeah, and then I'll become an item on your newscast like that guy the other night. What was his name? Phelps?"

"Do you mean that minister who renounced his faith on Sunday morning?" Tom asked.

"He didn't renounce his faith. He probably was a little more dramatic than he needed to be. I think he was just being honest about his interpretation of certain key theological concepts. All of a sudden, they were doing stories on him in the national newsmagazines. I don't want that to happen to me."

The bill lay awkwardly on the table.

"I'll get it this time," Tom said magnanimously. "You need to watch your money. You might be unemployed soon!"

"He laughs!" Jack grimaced. "This is serious."

"I know," Tom responded. "You're right. The world has changed. Most preachers I know do strike me as arrogant know-it-alls. Some of the people I work with actually believe that you guys are dangerous to the well-being of our enlightened society. But Jack, I can't help but think you're going to be all right. You're expressing honesty. And if there's one thing we need it's more honesty among preachers."

The thick air seemed almost hostile as they stepped outside. Dripping humidity was unusual for this part of the country. Jack felt lighter for having vented but no more sure of himself. His ankle twisted slightly as he stepped off the curb. The pavement was uneven and didn't make for a firm footing.

"Councilman Andrews was at church on Sunday," Jack said. "His wife has been coming for years, but now he's been showing up occasionally as well."

"He's been making a lot of noise about that break-in down the street from your church," Tom said.

"What kind of noise?"

"He's suggesting some kind of anti-environmentalist conspiracy."

"Fishing for votes, I'm sure."

Tom arrived at his car and climbed into the front seat. "I'm sure, too," he said to himself as he moved out into the traffic.

———

"I talked to the councilman's secretary," said Terri Jones. Thomas Newman's assistant was reliable. She was also attractive. Tom wondered which of these two qualities he appreciated more. "Just to get his comment on the record, and I quote, 'Mr. Andrews wishes to say that the recent break-in at the Green Valley Trust appears to be an invasion of this group's right to free speech. Powerful developers should not think that they can impose their will against the people's wishes. Despite all opposition, organizations will continue to have the opportunity to express their view that the beautiful natural areas surrounding our community must remain unspoiled.' Yadda, yadda, yadda."

"He doesn't come right out and accuse anybody, does he?" Tom asked.

"It's all innuendo and implication," Terri replied. "Nothing he could get sued over."

Tom laughed. "Philip Andrews: protector of the environment, opponent of big-business interests, friend to the common man."

"He knows the game, that's for sure," Terri laughed.

———

Jack Newman pulled his Ford Taurus into the church parking lot, nosing into the little wooden sign painted *PASTOR*. The car ran on a little after he turned the ignition off. He'd have to get somebody to look at that. He wondered, briefly, whether he could afford to shop for a new car. Driving an old car and living with less had never bothered him before. It had been enough for him to know that he was doing something important, that this was God's work. But now he was starting to wonder. His depression had grown since leaving the restaurant.

As Jack got out of the car a man approached him. His suit was newer than Jack's. Crisper. "Conrad Liu," the man said as he shook Jack's hand, pressing it firmly. "I'm with the P.D. Just asking questions regarding the break-in down the road. It's no big deal, of course. Just a simple thing, I'm sure. But the politicians—they get involved, and all of a sudden I'm treating a routine B and E as if it were a capital crime."

"It's okay," Jack said. "But I don't know that I have much to tell you."

"Did you see anything Sunday night?" asked Liu.

"I don't think so," Jack said. "I don't usually notice much come Sunday night," he admitted. "Sunday's a tough day for me."

"Okay," Liu said. "I just had to ask. Here's my card, by the way. Call me if anything comes to mind."

Jack examined the card as the policeman drove off in his unmarked car. "Conrad Liu, Detective." I think I'd like that job, Jack said to himself. Someone breaks into a building, you do your investigation, and you present the facts. Either the suspect did it or he didn't do it. If you have proof you prosecute, and if you don't you just keep moving forward. It's real stuff. Concrete. Not at all like preaching.

He walked into his office and pondered the stack of mail on his desk. His e-mail inbox was fuller yet. He didn't bother to check his voicemail, although the little green light was flashing obnoxiously. He opened the first e-mail message, an ad sent by a direct marketer. Junk mail, he said disdainfully. He noticed a magazine on top of his mail and thumbed through it. An article on culture caught his eye. Most of it pretty much followed his line of argument with Tom over lunch, he saw. But it was the conclusion that he really focused on.

The consequence of postmodern thinking could be characterized by three catch phrases, according to the article. The first—"Works for me"—struck Jack as on the mark. If nothing can be known for sure, then all people really have left is pragmatism. If it works, they'll hang on to it. If not, they'll jettison it.

The second statement, Jack thought, could be the one word that describes the whole postmodern attitude—"Whatever." Postmodern people don't make judgements. They're tentative in their conclusions. What else could they be? This all-purpose response allows them to take any direction that strikes their fancy, or none at all.

The final statement was—"Who cares." Jack noted that there was no question mark. It was given both as a statement as well as a question, he decided. On the one hand, postmodernists take a devil-may-care approach to life. "Who cares!" On the other hand, in their quieter moments they sincerely ask the question, "Is there anyone out there who cares about me?"

**———**

*"Works for me"*
*"Whatever"*
*"Who cares"*

It was discouraging. Jack looked around for his sermon scribblings for the coming Sunday before remembering he'd trashed them. He fished the notes out of the garbage can and tried to tackle the work, albeit without much enthusiasm. For a while, he looked through the notes he'd made, but his heart wasn't in it. Tomorrow, he told himself.

As he left the building, he noticed a mess of garbage under the back stairs. There were kids goofing around near those stairs last Sunday night, he remembered. Funny he hadn't been more concerned about that. Maybe he should call the detective and let him know about that. I'll call him first thing in the morning, Newman told himself.

Tom Newman set aside his concern for his brother as he looked into the Pinocchio nose of the camera.

"Five, four, three . . ."

Then he launched into his report. He was in his "trust me" mode.

". . . while most likely the work of petty thieves, Councilman Philip Andrews continues to raise the possibility that the break-in was deliberate. At this hour, the police are keeping all possibilities open. . . ."

Meanwhile, the pulpit stood in its customary place, oblivious to its master's ruminations. The sanctuary was dark and quiet, typical for a Monday afternoon. From the backside, the pulpit appeared disheveled. Visible only to the musicians and the pastoral staff was a mess of discarded worship bulletins and a glass of stale water. A tangle of wires and cords betrayed the mystery of modern electronics. The microphone was something of an indignity to the pulpit, actually. Such accommodation to contemporary convenience seemed to demean its ecclesial majesty. The podium rested in its midweek dormancy. Sunday would return as it always did, and the pulpit would again enjoy its prominence.

Jack Newman set his magazine down and struggled out of the chair. He walked over to the window and stood silently. In the distance, he could see the downtown architecture and the late afternoon traffic snaking its way to the suburbs.

What was he supposed to do now? This postmodern thing violated every principle and proposition of his homiletic training. He had been taught that the truth was outside of us, that God, objective and transcendent, existed independent from and unmoved by the vagaries and variances of contemporary life. What is more, he had been taught that the truth could be known and that God had made himself known. He was to explain the Word of God carefully so that people could know in their minds that life made sense, that there was purpose in the universe. He had been taught that people should be persuaded of these things and that persuasion was the purpose of preaching.

He wasn't so sure anymore. Persuading people seemed like an arrogant thing to do in a culture that distrusted one-size-fits-all truths. How could he continue to call for commitment to his own concept of Christ? It was conceit, wasn't it?

Could he ever again take his place behind the pulpit?

Elsewhere a man's pocket buzzed. He pulled out his cell phone and put it to his ear. The connection was bad, and the voice on the other end was crackly. "It's done." Then the line went dead.

# 2

# Theology for Preaching

Jack Newman sat motionless in the driver's seat, his hand on the key in the ignition. Turning the key would mean starting the car, which would mean driving to work, which would mean making a commitment to another week and another sermon. More out of habit than out of resolve, Jack started the car and eased it out into the traffic. He'd often said that he liked living close to the office so he didn't have to waste time commuting. Today, he might have liked a longer drive— much longer. In fact, Jack wasn't sure the commute to work could be *long enough* this particular Tuesday morning. He pulled into his parking spot next to Pastor Henry's familiar beige Impala. Henry had retired from pastoral ministry many years earlier. Unfortunately, retirement was unrealistic for a man of Jack's age.

---

"Yeah, I saw the news last night." Helen Lee was trying to sound busy. A few months ago, she'd told Stephen Lang she would handle some of the legal work for the Green Valley Trust pro bono. She didn't think it would amount to much, and it would give her a chance to portray a social conscience. But Lang, the director of the environmental agency, had been more demanding than she had expected. And now there was this break-in. Another headache, no doubt.

"So, what do you think?" Lang asked. "Could there've been a political motive behind it?"

"Anything's possible, Stephen," Helen said.

"So who are we talking about?" Lang asked. "Who could profit from this? Have you heard anything downtown?"

"I'm your lawyer, Stephen," Helen complained. "I'm not your political advisor."

"I've heard the mayor might be behind this." Lang wouldn't drop it. "We've been pushing him pretty hard. Maybe too hard. Maybe he sent someone to dig up dirt on us."

Reluctantly, Helen set aside the file she'd been working on and rubbed her eyebrows. The throbbing was back, building from the base of her neck. "Look, Stephen, nobody trusts the mayor. It's part of the game. Mayors aren't supposed to be trusted, right? After a while, even a good mayor begins to think that if everybody assumes he's a scoundrel, he might as well act like one. Was this guy behind it? I have no idea. Could he have done it? Of course he could have!" Helen Lee was warming to the subject. "You know," she said, "if we could prove it . . ."

---

Jack was fidgeting at his desk, laptop on, Bible software on the screen. He had gathered a selection of commentaries and a few pertinent theological texts. He arranged the books on his desk, opening each to the appropriate section. Stalling. If he could have thought about some other mindless thing, he would have done it—anything to postpone the inevitable a little while longer. Eventually, he would have to settle in and go to work. But, the reverend wasn't feeling very settled. I should get a can of Pepsi, he decided.

---

"How can they say this about me?" The mayor rolled the newspaper and flung it across his expansive office, grazing a lampshade and sending it spinning.

Here we go, thought Franklin Porter. Porter, rumpled advisor to the mayor since their early days in the fourth district, had seen the odd tantrum before. It could even be amusing at times. The paper lay accusingly on the floor open to the offending editorial. "Green Valley Break-In: Was Sims Involved?" read the tag line.

"I might as well have been there myself, the way they've got it," the mayor fumed.

"Wearing a ski mask and carrying a blackjack," Porter offered.

His Worship, Mayor Theodore Sims, was not amused. His boyish athleticism, an asset during campaigning, had faded with the years. This present anger, though, seemed to revive his youthful vigor. This was personal. "It's Andrews, isn't it? He's the one feeding them this garbage."

"It's likely. Of course, he's too smart to get his name attached to a story like this."

"I need to know how to respond," Sims said.

"Any chance we *are* involved in this?" Porter asked. "Not you. I mean someone in the organization. Maybe one of the staffers trying to get recognized?"

"How would I know?" Sims said. "If any of our people did this, it was a bonehead move. A sensitive project like this—publicity doesn't help us."

"What about Murphy?" Franklin Porter had never trusted Bill Murphy. For years he had been cautioning the mayor against aligning himself too closely with the owner of Dogwood Developments.

"Come on Ports, Murphy wouldn't do this. He's smart enough to know that these environmentalists are real believers. Something like this isn't going to slow them down. A break-in! It's crazy! Watergate stuff . . ."

---

Henry Ellis missed the pastorate. One year into retirement, he found himself looking for any kind of excuse to spend time at the church. It's hard to let go of the patterns of a lifetime, he admitted to himself. It was nice to not have to deal with the pressure of weekly sermon prep, the constant phone calls, the unmet expectations. It was just that he didn't know what else to do. Henry handled the church's prayer chain ministry and often came in early in the week to check the prayer cards people put in the offering. He also checked in with Pastor Jack.

Jack was grateful to hear him coming. "Sit down, Henry," Jack smiled. "Tell me about life after preaching!"

Henry noticed the familiar array of commentaries and study guides. "I just came in to check for prayer requests," he said. "I won't bother you. It looks like you're in the middle of your sermon."

"Nonsense," Jack said. "I'd love to spend a few minutes with you this morning. Maybe you can help me out of my funk."

"I'm afraid my counseling skills have grown rusty with disuse," Henry said. "That's your job now. You're supposed to counsel me."

"Actually, I'm serious," Jack said. "You're right. I'm supposed to take care of everyone else's problems. But what about me? You could help me, Henry," he said. "You know what it's like. You've been through this stuff. I could really use some of the wisdom of your experience."

"This sounds serious," Henry said. His heartbeat was accelerating perceptibly. It was nice to be needed. "What's the problem, Jack?"

"It's the sermon, actually," Jack said.

"Well, what's your text," Henry asked.

"It's not this sermon specifically," Jack said. "It's the business of preaching generally. I think I've lost my confidence."

"You're a fine preacher," Henry offered. "Janey and I deeply appreciate your faithful ministry of . . ."

"That's great," Jack interrupted. "But things have changed, Henry. When you were in your prime, people listened to you. They valued what you said. There was a certain authority that attached itself to the pulpit. Now, that authority has been reconstructed as arrogance. People don't believe in anything anymore, and I don't know what to do about it."

"But you believe, Jack," Henry said. "As a preacher, you know the power of God's Word preached. You know that God has promised to honor His Word, that it will not come back void."

"Actually," Jack admitted, "I'm not sure if I do believe. Wait, that's not right. I still believe that God exists. I'm just not sure that I can hear from him well enough to preach."

"What do you mean?"

"It's this whole postmodern thing." Jack wasn't sure that Henry was up to speed on postmodern philosophy, but he was positive the old guy knew his theology. "God's transcendent, right? He's wholly other—the indisputable sovereign, holy and unsullied by any stain of imperfection."

"Preach it," Henry smiled.

———

*Hermeneutics is both disenchanted and disenfranchised by the suggestion that there are no principles for right and wrong interpretation, only preferences.*

KEVIN J. VANHOOZER, *IS THERE A MEANING IN THIS TEXT?* 20.

"Okay," said Jack. "The problem is that I'm not any of those things. I'm riddled with imperfection. Just because I'm human, I'm locked into my particular moment in space and time. I'm fixated on the narrow concerns of my particular situation, philosophically speaking. And I'm the preacher! I'm supposed to try to help people hear from God. The problem is that as soon as I touch the Word of God or hear the voice of God, I mess it up. I put my fingerprints all over it and make it my own. I put the slant of my interpretation on it. The people have to get past my biases, my idiosyncrasies, and my sin." Jack's feelings were unrestrained by this time. His voice was getting louder. Half standing, half sitting, his words spit a bitter intensity. "The thing is, I'm convinced that more than ever people need to hear from God. We're getting hit from all sides with messages seeking to persuade us in one direction or forty-nine others. My voice is just one more added to the noise. Why would anyone listen to me? What's going to insure that my voice, my sermon is going to stand out above the others? What's the point . . . ?"

---

*Today if you live in New York City, you see 8,000 commercial messages a day.*

LEONARD SWEET, *SOULTSUNAMI*, 77.

"Whoa, Jack. Count to ten, my friend. Unball your fists." Henry leaned back in his chair and studied his young pastor. Jack, a little flustered and slightly embarrassed, was reeling himself back in. He rearranged himself in his chair and adopted the more familiar pastoral pose. This was a rare moment, Henry realized. Jack didn't often expose his feelings so openly.

"This postmodernism thing. This is new, right? The latest, hottest thing in philosophy?"

"Judging by the journal articles and book titles coming out lately, I'd say so," Jack said.

"It's not so new," Henry chuckled. "New name for it, maybe, but it's not unique to the current age. It's just that we weren't so quick to admit some of these things in my day. If anything, these 'postmodernists' are maybe just a little more honest about things that we in my era were too proud to admit."

Jack looked at Henry a little more intently.

---

*It was not good that the minister should be worshipped and made an oracle. It is still worse that he should be flattered and made a pet.*

PHILLIPS BROOKS, *ON PREACHING*, 66–67.

"I kind of liked being the voice of God for the people every Sunday," Henry confided. "You gotta admit, it's a pretty heady thing to have a crowd gather week in and week out to listen to you dispense the very wisdom of God. Every Sunday they would make their pilgrimage to the mountain of my pulpit, and I would give them what they wanted—pearls of wisdom, truth from God prepared and delivered from yours truly." Henry laughed. "They never paid me much in money, but they paid me richly in respect. Those people fed my hungry pride even as I fed their famished spirits. It was a pretty good deal."

"That kind of people aren't around much anymore," Jack said.

"It's a good thing, Jack," Henry said. "You don't need that kind of temptation. Your problem is much more honest than my pride."

No one spoke for several moments. The honesty of the moment hung heavily. A telephone rang in the distance; traffic hummed in the background.

"It's a problem," Henry admitted. "As a preacher, I was always telling people how the Bible was the Word of God, the objective truth for all time. But what does that really mean if we have to interpret it? I'd stand in the pulpit all the time, telling people what the text meant and how to interpret it correctly, knowing full well that if the people went two blocks down the street to another church, they might very well get an entirely different point of view."

"Getting a second opinion is all right for medical purposes, but it's not so good for preaching," Jack said.

"But that's the problem, isn't it!" Henry said. "Why do we need second opinions from doctors? Doctors are scientists, aren't they? They shouldn't have differences of opinion, but they do, because they understand that we really don't know all there is to be known."

"That reminds me of Dr. Suess," Jack said.

Henry looked surprised. It had been a terribly long time since he had seen the inside of a children's book.

"*On Beyond Zebra*," Jack said. "I used to read it to my kids. 'Said Conrad Cornelius O'Donnell O'Dell, my very young friend who was learning to spell, the A is for Apple, the B is for Bear, the C is for Camel, the H is for Hair . . .' The book describes a kid who thinks he knows it all. He's got a letter or a category for everything. He believes that he knows everything that's knowable."

"I think that kid was in my congregation," Henry laughed.

"Well, little Conrad has his comeuppance. There's a second child who's not so easily impressed. 'Then I almost fell flat on my face on the floor, '" Jack continued, "'when he picked up the chalk and drew one letter more. A letter I had never dreamed of before . . .' I still remember it," Jack said.

"This second kid has discovered a world 'beyond Zebra' where there are no categories for the kinds of things that can be discovered. 'So, on beyond Z! It's high time you were shown that you really *don't* know all there is to be known.'"

"I like that," Henry said.

"Well, it illustrates our dilemma, doesn't it," Jack said. "People hold our preaching suspect, because they know it's a big world out there. They know that God is bigger than our attempts to describe him. They know that life is complicated, and they don't trust anybody who claims to have it all sorted out."

"Even if the claim is founded on the Bible," Henry agreed.

"I feel as if it's hopeless," Jack complained.

The words hung in the air for a time. Henry resisted the urge to speak. A door closed loudly in the distance. Jack began to feel uncomfortable in the wooden chair. He would have to find some kind of a cushion. . . .

"It is hopeless," Henry said. "Hopeless. I didn't realize it early in my ministry. I was confident in my hermeneutics and my homiletics, and I was going to change the world by the breadth of my preaching. It wasn't until the end of my career in the pulpit that I really started to wonder how much of my preaching had been pure hot air. I know now that the problem is bigger than I was ever willing to admit. My arrogance notwithstanding, the one sure thing is that my personal charisma and my most persuasive rhetorical skills are not going to carry me very far."

Jack was surprised. He had no idea. Henry was a stalwart. He'd been preaching before Jack was even born. He couldn't imagine that Henry had ever felt this way. Jack sat straighter in his seat and focused more intently on the old man in front of him.

Henry continued, "It is hopeless, except . . ."

"Except what?" Jack asked.

"Except for the most wonderful, amazing, thing in the world. Except for the fact that God is alive and at work and that he has something to say even through humbled and broken-down preachers like you and me. This is God's project. It's what *he* is doing, and that's the one thing that gives me hope."

---

*Human reason cannot figure its way to such a God, since a God we could figure out, a God fitted to the categories of our understanding, would therefore not be transcendent in an appropriately radical sense. We can know the transcendent God not as an object within our intellectual grasp but only as a self-revealing subject, and even our knowledge of divine self-revelation must itself be God's doing.*

WILLIAM C. PLACHER, *THE DOMESTICATION OF TRANSCENDENCE*, 182.

Henry stood up and ambled over to the window. There were kids playing basketball in the schoolyard. Recess, he thought. He turned and looked at Jack. There was intensity in his gaze. "Let go of it, Jack. That's my advice," Henry said. "This is God's project, not yours. The most astounding thing I know is that our God is a self-revealing God. He isn't some disconnected deity leaving us to make things up as we go along. God speaks! He isn't silent!" Henry paused to let his words sink in.

"Remember your seminary theology, Jack? The doctrine of revelation? God is actively communicating his nature, his will, and his way every day the earth turns. It's not up to you to declare objective truth. It's God's project!"

Jack was impressed with Henry's passion, but the old guy was confusing him. "So you *do* think I should resign the pulpit?" Jack asked.

"No," Henry said. "No. No, by all means no." Henry grabbed his chair and dragged it around the desk so that he could sit alongside Jack. He rummaged through the stuff on the desk looking for a pen and a clean sheet of paper. "Tell me, Jack. First-year theology class. How does God reveal himself?"

"Through general revelation by means of creation," Jack said. Henry wrote the word "Initiation" on the paper in big block letters.

"God also revealed himself through his Son, Jesus Christ." Jack didn't have to think too hard. Though he wasn't used to recalling seminary lectures from fifteen years earlier, this was elementary stuff. Henry wrote the word "Incarnation" on the paper.

"A third way God speaks is through his Word, the Bible," Jack continued. Henry nodded his head as he carefully wrote the word "Inspiration" below the other two.

"Finally," Jack said, "God reveals his will through direction of the Holy Spirit."

"That's good," Henry said. "'A' for the day!" He wrote the word "Illumination" on the paper.

### Doctrine of Revelation

- ▶ Initiation
- ▶ Incarnation
- ▶ Inspiration
- ▶ Illumination

"These things all work together," Jack continued. "You can't claim that the Holy Spirit told you to go kill your mother-in-law when the Bible emphasizes the sanctity of life. These things work in concert with one another."

"My mother-in-law will be relieved," Henry said. "Although at her age . . ." The two men laughed. Henry began to write Scripture references on the paper beside the words he had written down. "Okay, we're getting somewhere with this. According to Genesis 1:26, we've all been created in the image of God. That means, among other things, that we are hardwired to hear from him and to recognize his voice when he speaks. Secondly, John 1:14 says that Jesus is the Word become flesh. That's actually a pretty good description of preaching: the Word of God enfleshed or lived out in real life. Second Timothy 3:16 says that all Scripture is breathed out by God. It comes literally from within him as an expression of his nature and his character. In other words, the Bible becomes foundational for people who want to know what God is saying. First Corinthians 2:13 tells us that the Holy Spirit sheds light on truth and helps us understand the mysteries of God's revelation."

"True enough," Jack said. "This is all basic stuff."

"Yes," Henry said. He was getting excited now. "But have you ever thought about the place of preaching in this construction? Preaching is when human beings, created in God's image, bear witness to the incarnate Christ as described in the inspired Scriptures, under the power and direction of the Holy Spirit."

"The whole thing converges in the act of preaching," Jack said. His engine was starting. He didn't have to convince people of the foundational truth of Scripture. He simply had to help them hear what God was saying and let God do the rest.

### Anderson's "Nutshell Definition of Preaching"

Preaching is helping people hear from God.

"Preaching is the point of integration for all four aspects of God's self-revelation," Henry summarized. "Preachers literally help people hear from God!"

---

The editorial in the morning paper unsettled Bill Murphy. While it was true that the spotlight hadn't turned his way yet, the president of Dogwood Developments took little comfort in it. What was the mayor up to? What was the councilman's angle? What could he do to protect himself? These stories had a way of growing. Gulping down his coffee, he looked around for the dog leash. He did some of his best thinking while walking the dog.

⸺⸻

Tom Newman, intrepid reporter, pulled his car up to the curb in front of the offices of the Green Valley Trust. Amazing, he thought, that a nondescript building like this could be the site of so much attention. He wanted to see the place for himself. Maybe he could learn something. Perhaps there would be some kind of clue. He felt a little silly, though. Tom had always sneered at those television dramas that turned every reporter into Bob Woodward investigating Watergate. But now, here he was snooping around just like on television.

A handwritten note on the window indicated that the offices were closed. He tried the door anyway and was surprised to find it unlocked. He entered tentatively, unsure just how far his journalistic license could take him. He didn't touch anything, just looked around, trying to get a feel for the place.

A political motive for the break-in made sense. It was hard to imagine that these offices held anything valuable enough to interest a garden-variety burglar. Surely, they couldn't expect to find money in a place like this. Green Valley was minor league. The Greenpeaces of the world sucked up the big donations. Smaller operations like Green Valley relied on scarce local money, which meant they tended to run on a shoestring. The brochures were not the glossy product of a New York advertising firm. They were printed on an inkjet and photocopied in-house. The posters on the wall were created by schoolchildren. "Green not Grey" read one. It was crayoned on fluorescent poster board.

"Hello, Tom," a voice said from the other side of a filing cabinet.

"Sounds like Conrad," Tom answered. If he had to be caught snooping on private property, he was certainly relieved that it was a friend who made the discovery. "I hope it's okay I'm here," Tom said "The door was open."

"No problem," said the detective. "Just don't mess things around."

"Eyes only," Tom agreed.

"So whaddaya think?" Conrad wasn't arrogant enough to discount the fresh eyes of an experienced investigator.

"Not sure," Tom answered. "I'm having trouble believing it's just a routine break-in. You gotta wonder about the politics of the thing." Liu grunted his response.

"Things don't appear to be messed up that badly, which would call into question the theory that this was the work of kids just coming in to vandalize the place."

"I think you're just looking for a story," the detective said. "Reporters are always trying to inflate routine business. Sells better, I guess."

"Well, whoever broke in here didn't come in to make a donation," Tom replied.

"I saw your newscast last night," Liu said. "You gave that councilman Andrews a big platform for his innuendoes, and now you're here looking for corroboration so you can keep the story alive."

"That's why you're the detective, Conrad. You don't miss a trick." Tom Newman noticed a file marked "Press" on a shelf in the corner. Forgetting his promise to look but not touch, he took the file down and blew a layer of dust off the cover. The file was filled with clippings from local newspapers—most of them old—probably everything written about the group for the last ten years. There were all the prepared statements, the staged protests, and the press conferences dutifully reported by willing beat reporters. Green Valley business didn't attract the first-string journalists, Tom noticed. The lobby had been busy and efficient in making its message known. In addition, there was the unsolicited news, public backlash evidenced by letters to the editor, and opinion pieces of varying lengths and fervor.

Wait a minute. Tom stopped at a picture of Philip Andrews. The picture was a couple of years old, taken at a campaign dinner during the politician's latest run for city council. Yet it wasn't so much the picture that grabbed his attention as it was the headline: "Candidate Raises Tough Questions for *Green Valley*." The article described Andrews's speech as a hard-hitting critique of the environmentalist opposition to urban development. "I'm all for clean water and healthy ecosystems," the candidate was quoted as saying. "But I'm also for well-paying jobs and healthy businesses. Organizations that want to protect our natural environment to the point where the average guy can't get a job anymore must be opposed, *and I'm the one who'll do it for you!*" That doesn't sound like the Andrews we know and love, Tom whispered to himself. Newman looked at the picture once again, holding it closer to his face. The grainy image of a smiling Bill Murphy of Dogwood Developments lurked in the background.

⸺◈⸻

Jack Newman wandered back to his office, shoeless as usual. He had decided years ago that he worked more efficiently in sock feet. At least it made him more comfortable, and he liked to be comfortable when he settled in to work.

The discussion with Henry had been encouraging. Enough, at least, to stimulate a fresh start on his sermon. Jack returned to his desk and sat down with a sigh. Helping people hear from God. He liked the idea, he had to admit. For too long, he had bought into the idea that he was an information salesman, trying to get people to buy ideas and concepts that they appeared to have little interest in or use for. At other times, he had served more as a homiletical archaeologist. The archaeologist spends time digging around in the dust emerging with ancient treasures that have little contemporary, practical value. They hold their discoveries up to the world and say, "Look at what I found. Isn't it precious! Isn't it beautiful! Isn't it old!" And the rest of the world yawns and says, "Looks like a piece of broken pottery to me." As a preacher, Jack felt like that a lot of the time. Preachers would dig into the dust of the ancient text and find some truth from long ago and far away that looked for all the world like broken pottery to their congregations. Yes, ancient artifacts are valuable and important, but to people caught up in the struggle of immediate issues such products seem hopelessly irrelevant.

Preaching as archaeology was unsatisfying to Jackson Newman. He had to know that when he opened his mouth the people would recognize he had a message from God—uniquely crafted for their moment and position in time. Last month, Tom had tickets to a Lakers-Knicks play-off game. Jack had found himself watching the fans as much as the game. The way they sat on the edge of their seats in the dying seconds of the game, the way they seemed hungry for every drive and dunk—these people ate it up. They stood and cheered. They slumped in their seats in disappointment. They rose in anger at the referees. They responded as one to the whole gripping environment. They were completely and utterly engaged in the event. And all the while, Jack was thinking, Why couldn't my preaching be like this? Oh, not with all the hype, the furry mascots and the bare-tummied cheerleaders. But with the same intensity of expectation, the same joyful anticipation. It might not always be pretty, but at least there would be life and energy.

And why not, Jack concluded. After all, the Bible is the Word of God. It's not just some static body of information. The Bible is a living, breathing, dynamic presentation of the voice and message of God in real time. Studying Scripture wasn't about clarifying what God *said* thousands of years ago. It is about listening to what God is saying in the here and now. Preaching, then, would be much more of an event in time, as opposed to the presentation of information outside of time. It would be unrepeatable, unpublishable even, because it would offer whatever it was that God was saying through *this* text, to *these* people, at *this* time. I could preach the exact same manuscript, word for word, to the same group of people a week later, Jack reflected, and it would be a new sermon. People change and things happen. God speaks into time, not above it.

———

*We should be praying that God will raise up a new generation of Christian communicators who are determined to bridge the chasm; who struggle to relate God's unchanging Word to our ever-changing world; who refuse to sacrifice truth to relevance or relevance to truth; but who resolve instead in equal measure to be faithful to Scripture and pertinent to today.*

JOHN R. W. STOTT, *BETWEEN TWO WORLDS*, 144.

Jack recalled seminary homiletics—the endless discussion of text and today—and how they all learned to bridge the so-called gap between the ancient text and the contemporary situation. Maybe the gap has been overplayed, Jack wondered. Maybe I've actually been creating distance for my listeners by boring them with my archaeological forays in the dust. Maybe it isn't a matter of balancing text and today. Maybe the text *is* today. People haven't changed all that much, Jack reminded himself. The concerns of the Colossians are not all that different from the contemporary concerns of my congregation, he decided. The events are different, but the stuff is the same, and it's all about God speaking. Not what he *said*, but what he's *saying*.

Jack was breathing heavily. It surprised him to feel so vital and alive.

The secretary removed the earpiece from her Dictaphone. She could say this for her boss; he sure knew how to get on the right side of an issue. She had been principle secretary to Philip Andrews since he had first announced his candidacy, and she'd always admired his political instincts. He always seemed to know exactly how to play things. This letter to the editor was just another example. They had talked about the timing for his run at the mayor's chair. That time appeared to be ripening.

Where was that article? Jack asked himself. He kept a pile of articles and "stuff to be filed" on top of his cabinet, and the pile was growing. The idea was that, whenever he read material that was of value to him, he would file it away so he could find it again later. The filing part never actually seemed to happen, however. His filing system was more of a piling system, which made the whole exercise almost useless.

There it is! Jack pulled a dog-eared copy of the journal *Priorities* from near the bottom of the stack. The author had suggested a simple little model for thinking about communication. It struck Jack that it might be helpful in his attempt to communicate in the climate of postmodernism.

The article suggested that there are two primary issues to address whenever a speaker intends to communicate persuasively. The first issue is *authority* and the second is *apprehension.* Authority has to do with the foundation on which the message rests. "Oh yeah, who says?" is a legitimate question. Listeners have a right to question that foundation, because an argument is only as strong as the base it's built on.

The author suggested that there were two forms of authority a speaker could appeal to. One is *objective* authority. This refers to standards or values that stand outside of the listener or speaker as unquestioned givens. That the sky is blue or that two plus two equals four is, for all practical purposes, beyond question. An argument based on such propositions would appear to be firmly established.

The other form of authority available to the speaker is *subjective* authority. This is the listener's own sense of what is and what isn't. Every auditor has a grid of experiences and assumptions that have developed over time into an intricate filter. Everything he or she hears must pass through this filter in order to be verified as true and as worthy. It's why a listener can say, "That makes sense to me," or "I can buy that." What this means is that the message fits the listener's experience closely enough to be affirmed.

### Authority

Objective—Subjective

Jack chewed on the ideas for a moment. He thought about the sermon he had preached last month on the Ten Commandments. "Thou shalt not steal," for example. What's the authority for a proposition like that? Objective authority, he decided, would be the textual foundation for the message. Don't steal! "Oh yeah, who says?" God says, that's who. God created you. He gets to decide what is and what isn't, and he says don't steal. End of story.

---

*God said it. I believe it. That settles it.*

UBIQUITOUS 1970S BUMPER STICKER.

That's actually not bad, Jack concluded. God says. That puts the "author" back into the concept of authority. How could you find a firmer authority than the command of the creator?

Yet as he thought about the message that he had preached, he realized that he had been working with a different kind of authority as well. Don't steal! "Oh yeah, who says?" Well, Jack remembered himself saying, *you* do. You know you shouldn't be stealing. Thieves can't be trusted. Our society is founded upon some basic principles like property laws. If we can't trust one another to respect private property, the very underpinnings of culture will be weakened. Your family will come to lose trust in you. You could even end up in jail. You could lose everything of value to you. You know from your own experience that you shouldn't take what doesn't belong to you.

And the listener says, "That helps me. I can agree with that." Subjective authority, Jack concluded.

The second category mentioned in the article was *apprehension.* This one was a little easier for Jack to understand. Apprehension was not about fear. It was about encouraging listeners to grab hold of the truth and to make it their own. When a police officer *apprehends* a suspect, it means that he literally takes hold of the subject physically, slaps handcuffs on, and hauls the culprit into jail. That, the author said, is what the speaker wants the listener to do with the material being presented. The speaker wants the listener to buy into the material and to make a conscious and secure commitment to it. "OK. How do I help you?" the preacher asks. "How can I encourage you to grab hold of this and make it your own?"

There are two ways to try and accomplish this, the article said. One is by means of *cognition* and the other is by means of *intuition.*

### Apprehension

Cognitive—Intuitive

Cognitive apprehension is achieved by explaining things. The speaker strives to make things clear and concise. The material is presented in such a way that the listener understands logically and reasonably how it works. It's a 'head' issue. If the explanation is convincing enough, the listener will buy in.

Intuitive apprehension is about experiencing things. The speaker tries to help the listener *want* to respond positively. Apprehension is gained by encouraging the listener to feel the right things and to be moved emotionally by the message. It's a 'heart' concern. If the presentation is compelling enough, again, the listener will take hold of it.

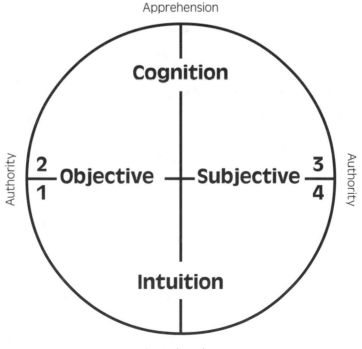

Jack realized the parallels to preaching. In his "Thou shalt not steal" sermon, Jack remembered that he had spent most of his time explaining the message to his listeners. He was careful to break down the text and to make the semantic connections and the technical-word meanings clear to the listeners. While that was helpful, he realized that he could have done some other things—perhaps tell a story about a real-life person ("Uncle Frank the kleptomaniac") who had lost people's trust because of an addiction to thievery. There were probably many ways, he realized, that he could encourage the listener to respond more positively to the message. He just needed to emphasize less cognitive approaches to apprehension.

The secret, the article said, is integration. That made sense to Jack. Integration is not about compromise. It's not even about balance. Things can be in balance even when they're weak, as long as they're equally weak. You could have two flat tires that are in balance with one another, but they're not going to get you anywhere. And compromise is about making hard sacrifices to unite competing views.

———

*The test of a first-rate intelligence is the ability to hold two opposed ideas in the mind at the same time, and still retain the ability to function.*

F. SCOTT FITZGERALD, QUOTED IN JAMES C. COLLINS
AND JERRY I. PORRAS, *BUILT TO LAST,* 45.

Integration is different. It requires no such sacrifice. Among the root words for integration is *integer* (a whole number) or *integrity*. Integration, therefore, is where two disparate substances are united in such a way that the essential nature of each of the substances is not compromised in any way. In other words, it is a matter of "both/and" instead of "either/or". A presentation can feature both subjective and objective authority, both cognitive and intuitive apprehension, simultaneously.

Jack realized he hadn't got a whole lot done on the sermon yet, but he was beginning to get a clearer sense of what he had to do. As a preacher he had to offer an explanation of the text, but that didn't mean he couldn't speak to the listeners more emotively, taking into consideration their perspectives at the same time. Emphasizing the listeners' experiences would not have to come at the expense of explanation. Postmodern people might respond to a more intuitive presentation, Jack thought. Thinking about the sermon more holistically couldn't hurt!

—————

The television was on when Jack returned home later that evening. Strange. No one seemed to be in the house. He walked over to the thermostat and turned it up a few notches. He expected to be home for the rest of the night, and he wanted it to be warm. He wandered over to the den and sat down in front of the television to watch the evening news, but nothing seemed to catch his interest.

He noticed his Bible sitting off to the side. Picking it up, he reread the text he'd settled on for that Sunday's sermon: Colossians 1:24–29, ". . . to them God has chosen to make known . . . the glorious riches of this mystery. . . ." The idea of the mystery of the gospel had always appealed to him.

Just then, he heard his brother's voice on the television. Jack looked up. There was Tom looking as dignified as ever in his tailored jacket and his hundred-dollar tie. He's probably wearing jeans underneath that desk, Jack smirked. "Arrests have been made in the burglary at Green Valley Trust," Tom intoned. "Two local men have been taken into custody. The police are offering no motive for the crime at this time."

# 3

# First Stage: Discovery
## THE MESSAGE

Conrad Liu looked hard into the eyes of the two young men standing in front of him. There wasn't much to find, he decided. Either these young men had been through the routine before, or they had unusually vacant temperaments, especially the older one. Liu had never understood fashion. They could both fit into one pair of those jeans, he decided. And what's with wearing a tuque in the middle of summer? Let's see how they look in orange jumpsuits. Liu allowed himself a little smile.

The detective had a feel for these guys. He had seen the type before. Sure, a lot of people would try to turn this into something political, but he wasn't having any of it. He would investigate, at least to satisfy the bosses and the media, but he was sure nothing would come of it. These guys just didn't look like political types. Everybody's always trying to make something out of nothing, he thought. People are looking for conspiracies in every little thing that comes across a police blotter. Most of the time, it's just a game, of course. Everyone's just trying to have a bigger profile.

Still, the question of motive was unanswered.

He'd have to be careful, Bill Murphy decided. Perception is reality, and if people got the idea somehow that he was involved in break-ins and ridiculous things like that, he could kiss his new golf course good-bye. He didn't understand why developers like him were always being painted as the bad guys. A lot of people like golf, he reminded himself. It's a civilized game for civilized people. He wished a few more of those civilized people would speak up every now and then. Why was it always the 'granola people' who got all the good press, prejudicing the public against his plans?

For the twenty-third time that afternoon, he walked over to the scale model of the course laid out in the corner of his office. He imagined himself hitting off the cliff-side tee box on the signature eighteenth hole. The condominiums cut into the side of the cliff would have an extraordinary view. He could almost hear the creek gurgling down across the common-area greenbelt.

Yes, he'd have to be careful. The donation couldn't be too large or too obvious. This was tricky. He didn't want it to seem as if he was buying positive press. He was, of course—or at least he was trying to. He'd write a modest personal check made out to the Green Valley Trust. A day or two later, he'd casually let it be known that, as a personal contributor to environmental causes such as Green Valley, he was as disheartened as everyone else about the break-in and would call on the police to get to the bottom of the case without delay. The environmentalists would really choke on that one, especially Stephen Lang. But if he could display the right amount of sincerity, he might actually be able to pull it off.

How big a check? Two hundred dollars was probably about right. The play had to be subtle and not flashy. He signed his name and tore the check out of a leather binder with gold embossing on the cover. He closed the book and placed it back in his desk drawer. Writing checks was useful when you wanted to leave a record. Good thing I covered that other matter with cash, he thought smugly.

"You've reached the desk of Tom Newman," the answering machine droned.

"Newman. Franklin Porter, Mayor Sims aide, here," he said brusquely. "We need to talk. The mayor needs a friendly ear—*exclusive.* Call me." Porter hung up and paused for a moment. He shook his head and walked away, a little smirk turning up the corners of his mouth.

—⟨⟨⟨⟨ ⟩⟩⟩⟩—

Tom Newman couldn't answer his phone because he was on the other line talking to his brother. They hadn't talked this much in years, he thought to himself. The lunch they'd shared on Monday had been like a window opening on an early spring day. The honesty they'd shared that afternoon had stimulated something good. He liked talking to Jack, and Jack appeared to enjoy talking to him.

"So where are you right now?" Jack wanted to know.

"At the office. Believe it or not, I'm not always out on some glamorous assignment. Where are you?"

"I'm on my cell." As if to emphasize the fact, the line crackled as Jack drove under a bridge. "Sorry about that. I'm back."

"Where are you off to today?" Tom asked.

"The hospital. I've got my traditional pastor's hat on this morning. I don't do as much of it as I used to, but there's still a core of people in the congregation who look to me for a regular personal visit."

"That must be frustrating," Tom suggested, "sipping tea with senior citizens and the like."

"You know, I actually don't mind it," Jack replied. "Oh, I'm glad everybody doesn't expect it, or I'd lose my mind. But I've seen some great things happen when I've tried to encourage people over time."

"You're just a traditionalist at heart," Tom chided.

"Actually, I'm starting to think that I am," Jack laughed. "I had a long talk with Henry Ellis yesterday. I really respect the way that he was able to represent God in the way he carried himself inside the pulpit and outside it. I'm feeling a little nostalgic for that old-time pastor stuff today, I guess."

"A little nostalgia never hurt anyone."

"Actually," Jack said, "talking to Henry really got me thinking about my preaching. For the last few years, I've had this idea that I was supposed to be really creative and contemporary in my preaching style. The guys who are writing the books today, and the guys who are preaching on the radio . . ."

"No," Tom complained. "Don't be listening to those guys."

"They're not so bad," Jack allowed. "Like I said, a lot of them are really trying hard to be heard by the average guy. Sermons these days will offer you, 'Seven keys to a more effective family life,' or 'Three ways to overcome stress in your life.'"

"That sounds more like a magazine cover than a sermon," Tom observed. He was leaning back in his office cubicle. It was almost lunchtime, and he decided that he didn't mind if someone found him relaxing on the job.

"That's what I wanted to say," Jack said. "A lot of the preaching I hear has been dumbed down to the lowest common denominator, and while I like a contemporary feel to preaching, I don't want to insult people's intelligence either."

"That was never a problem with the preaching I remember," Tom said.

"I know," agreed Jack. "Old-time preachers weren't always the most exciting people to listen to, but they did have something to say. And there are still some of them out there, too. They're busy trying to hold the line against homiletical weakness. They're parsing an extra verb and pounding their pulpits with a little more gusto. They're giving the people the Word of God as if it were foul-tasting medicine. 'Here, take this,' they say. 'It's good for what ails you.' But fewer and fewer people are showing up to fill their prescription."

"On the other hand," Jack continued, "you've got these young guys. They know how to dress and how to tell a great story. They've got the great music, the great show, and the great crowd, but they don't necessarily have anything to say. They've let go of Scripture so, while they've learned how to communicate effectively within the contemporary situation, they don't have a message that's worth committing your life to."

"I don't think I'd want to listen to either of the two," Tom allowed.

"Neither would I," Jack agreed. "I keep asking myself, why do I have to choose? Why do I have to limit myself to only one of these approaches?"

━━━━━━━

*How one might integrate the two perspectives of expository preaching is worthy of exploration. Is there a middle ground to the two extremes of text-orientation? Does such a middle ground necessitate theological or communicative compromises, or both?*

KEITH WILLHITE, "AUDIENCE RELEVANCE AND RHETORICAL ARGUMENTATION IN EXPOSITORY PREACHING," 261.

"Refuse to choose!" Tom cheered.

"Isn't it at least theoretically possible that I could take a page from Henry's generation and offer good solid, authoritative meat from the Word of God, but do it in a creative way that has life and passion and imagination?"

"I don't see why not," Tom assured his brother.

Jack's cell was breaking up. "Hold on Tom, I just pulled into the hospital, and I'm getting some static again."

"Just don't take the phone inside," Tom warned. "They get really excited if you try to use it inside. It messes up some of their equipment."

"I'm in no rush."

Both brothers paused for a moment, trying to find the thread of their earlier conversation. "I was just saying, I don't think you should have to choose between depth of content and relevance of style," Tom said.

"I don't either. In fact, I'm convinced that if I could find a way to integrate the two, I might really have something to offer postmodern listeners."

"Sounds good," Tom said. "Speak to both their heads and their hearts." He was fishing a sandwich from the side pocket of his briefcase.

"Now, I just have to figure out how to do it," Jack sighed. "Anyway, how are things moving along on the break-in story. I hear they caught a couple of kids."

"Not kids, really. Early twenties."

"How did they find them?"

"The usual way. They couldn't keep their mouths shut. I guess when it became such a big media story, they felt they had to get some credit. So, one of them shot his mouth off to a friend, and you know how it goes from there. Things get around."

"That's good," Jack said. "I wonder if they were the ones I heard outside the church on Sunday night."

"Probably were. The police found footprints in the dirt behind your back stairwell that matched the suspect's shoes. I'm surprised you haven't heard about that yet. The police only knew to look there because of what you told them."

"It would only be circumstantial anyway, wouldn't it?"

"Circumstantial, yes, but they have another witness. Your testimony would corroborate what they already know. It's important, because it puts them in the area at the right time. They'll probably want you to come in and make a formal statement."

"I could do that," Jack said. "Maybe it'll help to quiet things down a little. The political rhetoric has been getting a little thick lately."

"Maybe." Tom was noncommittal. "I was nosing around the Green Valley offices yesterday, and I found some things that got me wondering about your new parishioner Philip Andrews. Seems he's been flip-flopping on this environmental issue."

"Stop," Jack said in mock horror. "A politician who changes his mind? This is news! Quick, someone. Get a journalist. Oh wait, you *are* a journalist!"

"You're hilarious, Jack." Tom took a moment to wipe a bit of peanut butter off his cheek. "Seriously, Andrews gave a strong pro-development speech during the campaign. Not a lot of people remember that, but I did some checking. Dogwood Developments was a major donor to his campaign fund."

"Bill Murphy must be pretty upset that he's been so critical of his company, then."

"Well, maybe not," Tom said. "I did a little more research on Andrews's voting record, and it's a strange thing. He's voted with the developers on every single issue before city council—even the vote

on that strip mall they wanted to build on that site near Pender's Cross-
ing last year."

"That was the heritage site, wasn't it? I thought that vote was
unanimous."

"Not at first. Andrews was the only one to vote in favor of the proposal. They decided to take a second vote in order to be able to make
it unanimous. Looks better in the paper that way. Andrews held out
for as long as he could, but eventually he agreed to abstain. I'm guess-
ing he made some kind of a side deal in order to change his vote."

"And now, here he is speaking out for the poor downtrodden environmentalists as if he's been with them all along."

"The man's a hypocrite. He changed his public message, but his
voting record hasn't changed a bit. It is as if Bill Murphy has been doing
all his voting for him. It's a nice trick," Tom said. "Andrews needs
both constituencies. The developers have the money, and the public
has the votes. But he's astute, you see. Public attitudes have shifted,
so Andrews had to find a way to play to the voters without alienating
his money men. At least, that's my theory."

"The man's not a hypocrite," Jack suggested. "He's simply a pragmatic postmodernist."

"I guess. It probably is a sign of the times when a man's actions
and words don't have to be congruent. I just don't trust him, and for
me it raises questions about the whole thing. I suspect the implications
are more than political. There are too many people making too much
noise." Tom noticed that the newsroom was getting noisier. People
were starting to return from lunch. "Anyway, I'd better get some work
done here. I've got to call city hall. The mayor wants to bare his soul.
Maybe I'll send him to you. You can hear his confession."

"Wrong denomination, Tom. I don't do confessions."

"Well, then maybe I'll send him to Conrad Liu. I'll talk to you later.
Hope your sermon goes well on Sunday."

"Well, offerings have been way up lately," Jack responded, "so,
whether or not the sermon is any good, at least I know I'll get paid."

Helen Lee, the Green Valley lawyer, put down the newspaper and called Stephen Lang. "You can call off the dogs, Stephen. It's been all over the news. The front page, even. They caught the guys that broke into your offices. Sounds routine to me."

"It would have been a lot more fun if the mayor had been involved," Lang replied.

"Are you in this for fun, Stephen? I thought you were a true believer—a die-hard, sour-faced soldier for the cause," Lee teased him.

"I'm not sure I want to drop it all quite yet, Helen," Lang said. "There's got to be some mileage we can get out of this story before it goes away."

"That's what I love about him," Helen sighed, as she pressed the "End" button on her cell. There was always a little extra.

—⟨⟨⟨·⟩⟩⟩—

"So Franklin, *mea culpa* from the mayor? Is he growing tired of high office? Looking forward to a little enforced leisure? I hear they're softer on people who confess." Tom Newman actually liked talking to the mayor's aide.

"Ratings, my friend. You can promote the interview all day long. At six P.M. they'll all be sitting on their couches like birds on a telephone wire, ready to be reassured by the soothing presence of His Worship."

"What does the mayor want?" Tom asked. "You know I'll ask the tough questions."

"The tougher the better. The mayor comes off looking more sympathetic that way. He's got nothing to hide, Tom."

"I'll be there first thing in the morning."

"We'll have the coffee on," Porter said.

—⟨⟨⟨·⟩⟩⟩—

Jack found himself back at the office a little earlier than he'd expected. The woman he'd gone to visit in the hospital had been released. Should have gone yesterday, he murmured. Used to be with serious surgery you could count on a person staying in the hospital for a good long time to recover. Apparently, it had been decided that people heal faster at home, which meant the pastor had to be on the ball to fit the obligatory hospital call in. I hope I don't get any nasty phone calls over this one, Jack thought.

At any rate, he was happy to be digging into his sermon again. He'd always enjoyed the exegetical part of sermon preparation. He liked to work with a yellow legal pad. It was nothing for him to knock off ten or fifteen pages of notes in one good morning, looking at the original languages, reading the commentaries, doing mechanical layouts. He realized that he probably went overboard with this kind of work sometimes, but he enjoyed it. Jack had played around with other approaches to preaching. He'd tried the typical topical approaches. He'd gone the seeker route. He'd explored narrative preaching and other more innovative models (some of which he'd never actually understood). He'd even turned to buying sermon outlines over the Internet during a particularly desperate period about seven months ago. Yet, he kept coming back to biblical preaching. If, as Pastor Henry said, preaching was helping people hear from God, then what better place to go than to God's Word.

---

*Topical sermons are like topical anesthetics. They don't go deep.*

ROBERT FARRAR CAPON, *THE FOOLISHNESS OF PREACHING*, 63.

Some might say that the Bible was too difficult for people to understand without a lot of explaining. They might also say that the preaching has to be relevant to people's contemporary needs. But it had always been Jack's contention that the Bible was relevant—inherently relevant. It was God's Word, after all. What could be more relevant than the word of the Creator to his creatures! Sure a preacher might have to work a little harder in the book of Leviticus than in the gospel of John. Yet, that didn't mean the Leviticus text was unpreachable. Jack believed that every part of the Bible was God's Word and was, therefore, relevant and applicable to contemporary life. Founding one's sermon directly on the Scriptures, he believed, was a sure way to develop authority and to offer the listener something truly and ultimately meaningful.

He'd always looked on it as a challenge to see how he could take a text and find a way to communicate it so that contemporary people would grab hold of it and appreciate it. That, of course, was the problem. While he was giving people the Bible, the congregation was appearing less and less interested. Was it possible there was something wrong with the way he was doing it? he asked himself. He didn't think that he wanted to abandon his biblical approach to preaching.

---

*Against boredom the only defense is again being biblical. If a sermon is biblical, it will not be boring.*

KARL BARTH, *HOMILETICS*, 80.

His text for the current Sunday, Colossians 1:24–29 would provide a challenge, he decided. He'd already developed a sizable stack of exegetical notes. It was an interesting text. The idea of the *mystery* of the gospel had always appealed to him. It made the gospel sound appropriately exotic. He found Paul's personal passion for preaching to be encouraging—compelling even. There's a sermon here somewhere, he assured himself.

Jack thumbed through the stack of well-inscribed, lined yellow sheets. The problem he had was the same problem he had every week. The gap between exegesis and exposition is massive. He was never quite sure what to do with it all, once he was finished taking notes. How do you get from hermeneutics to homiletics, from this mess of notes to a sermon people will actually be interested in listening to?

Maybe I should go for a walk, he thought. Sometimes a change of physical posture helped stir the juices. He looked out the window and decided against the idea. It looked like rain, and he'd left his umbrella at home. He didn't feel like going out and getting wet just for the sake of some sermonic inspiration. The kids across the street were playing street hockey. The rain didn't seem to be bothering them. It's amazing how that game has caught on, he thought. Jack could remember when they used to play stickball in the very same lot. I should go out and see if they'll let me play sometime.

Looking back to his desktop, Jack's eye came to rest on the *Priorities* article that he'd been reading the day before. It struck him that maybe there was a way he could configure all his data so the step toward preaching wouldn't seem quite so ominous. Perhaps he was trying to make the transition to the sermon before he was ready. He pondered the situation for a while. Preaching is helping people hear from God, he reminded himself. Well then, what is it that God's saying?

## First Stage: Discovery

—The Message—
What is God saying through this text to these people at this time?

It was common in Jack's denominational tradition to use the terms 'sermon' and 'message' interchangeably. Maybe the two terms needed to be distinguished, he began to think. Perhaps the preacher needs to determine what the message actually is before settling down to build a sermon that would communicate that message. Perhaps he ought to discover the message before he tried to construct the sermon. Good thinking, Jack congratulated himself.

So what is the message from this text anyway? Jack questioned. He said it again, out loud this time. "What is God saying through this text to these people at this time?" No use knowing what God said last week to some other group of people. There's been enough sermons preached to people who are never there—like the president or "those people," whoever they might be. What is God saying through this passage to *these people* today? If he could beam in on the message that

God intended, he'd be in a better position to develop an effective sermon later in the process. He thought about the model in the article
he'd read the day before. He took a sheet of paper out of the blue recy-
cling box he kept under his desk, turned it over to the clean side, and
drew the model. It was already printed in the magazine, but he wanted
to draw it for himself, one piece at a time. He wanted to be sure he
understood the implications. He drew the horizontal line first, repre-
senting authority. On the left side of the line, he was about to write
the word *objective*. Instead, Jack pondered for a moment then wrote
the word *text* in its place. On the right side of the line, where the word
*subjective* appeared in the article, Jack wrote the word *today*. Next,
he drew the vertical line. This line represented apprehension. Where
the author had written *cognitive*, Jack wrote the word *explanation*.
On the lower half of the line, where the word *intuitive* had been offered in the article, Jack wrote the word *experience* instead.

Jack stopped to consider what he'd done. Not that there was any-

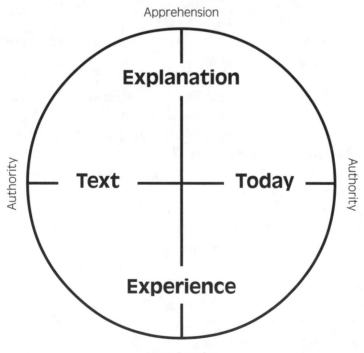

thing wrong with the author's original words, but Jack always preferred to do things his own way. It gave him a sense of ownership.

He went back and read what the author had said about integration. "Integration is where two disparate substances are united in such a way that the essential nature of each of the substances is not compromised in any way." So, how do I integrate these components so they make me a better preacher? That was the bottom-line question, wasn't it?

The phone rang. He let the answering machine handle it. He seldom did that. Pastoral guilt told him to answer every call. Not this time. For once, he would put his sermon first.

There were four quadrants in the model. Jack decided to label them. He put a number one in the bottom, left-hand corner quadrant. Moving clockwise, he numbered the rest of the quadrants as well, two through four.

Okay, now what? he asked himself.

The phone rang again. This time he didn't even hear it.

———

Conrad Liu's phone was ringing, too. Unlike the homiletically entranced pastor, the detective answered the call. "Conrad Liu here."

"Detective, this is Philip Andrews calling. I'm a member of city coun—"

"I know who you are, sir. You've been kind of hard to miss lately."

"I guess I have been on the news a lot these days."

"Well, you'll have to find another issue to ride, I'm afraid. We're just about to put the Green Valley file to bed."

"Actually, Detective, that's why I called."

"I figured," Liu said under his breath. He pushed the *record* button on his phone.

"I want to say that we on city council have the highest regard for the work you're doing. Our police force is integral to the safety and security of our . . ."

"Actually, I don't need the speech, sir. We're all pretty aware of the importance of our work around here."

"There's more to this story," Andrews blurted.

"There usually is."

"Detective *Liu*, is it? Do you really think that these young men acted alone? You'll forgive me, but I think I've learned a little bit about human nature during my years in public life. Where's the motive for this crime? There wasn't any money, was there? There wasn't any reason . . ." Andrews was talking like a kindergarten teacher patiently explaining the laws of nature to a five-year-old.

"Why do you care, sir, if you don't mind my asking?" Liu forcibly interrupted. "What's your part in all of this? Why don't you just let us do our job?"

"Look to the mayor's office."

Silence.

"Anything more you want to say about that, Mr. Andrews? I believe you just made a pretty serious accusation about a prominent civic politician."

"Look, Detective, I won't try to fool you. My motive is pretty obvious. I'm not proud of it, but the mayor's my opponent. I think he's dirty, and I don't want him to get away with it. I'm telling you, there's a much bigger case here than you seem to realize. Look to the mayor."

"Again, sir, do you have any proof?"

"Not that you could use in a court of law."

"Well, respectfully then, sir, you don't have anything."

"The court of public opinion isn't so stringent about the rules of evidence," Andrews threatened.

"Your walking on dangerous ground, you know."

"Ask the Mayor. I'm a dangerous guy." Slowly, decisively, the city councilman put the phone back in the cradle. "I'm a dangerous guy," he said again, as if to try and convince himself.

———

Jack walked down to the church kitchen and retrieved a Pepsi from the fridge where he maintained a supply. It was his one vice. We all get our caffeine one way or another, he thought to himself. At least I don't drink twelve cups a day like some coffee drinkers I know.

He returned to his desk and took another run at his project. *Integration*, he reminded himself. Okay, quadrant one. Here's where we think about text and experience. Texts aren't created simply to be understood. Texts are made to be experienced. Texts are about real people who live in real time. There's a story behind every text. Surprising though it might be, even the epistle of Romans was written to real people who lived in ancient Rome. Understanding the original story could help listeners identify their story in the light of the grand story of God's activity among people here on earth. The human element in the text could prove crucial in developing a connection for contemporary listeners. Jack wrote the words "What's the story?" in the first quadrant. It's a good place to start, he decided.

---

*Of all the ways we communicate with one another, the story has established itself as the most comfortable, the most versatile—and perhaps the most dangerous.*

ROBERT FULFORD, *THE TRIUMPH OF NARRATIVE,* X.

Quadrant two came a little easier to him. Jack felt as if he was on familiar ground when it came to thinking about the explanation of the text. He didn't have to think very long before he wrote the words "What's the point?" in the appropriate space. Even narrative texts usually have points. If the Bible really is a means by which God reveals truth, then the propositional intention of the text ought to be given full consideration. Of course, this is usually the bread and butter of traditional evangelical preaching. I'm usually all over this one, he said to himself.

---

*I know that if we think the wrong thing about God it will not be long before we start feeling and doing the wrong thing as well. Propositional truth matters. Propositional truth about God matters supremely.*

IAN PITT-WATSON, *A PRIMER FOR PREACHERS,* 98.

Moving to the third quadrant, integrating explanation and today, proved a little more challenging, however. The difficulty is that the cognitive reasoning of contemporary people will rarely match up with the propositional intention of the text. Whether it was the stimulus of the caffeine or that of the ideas, Jack was thinking sharply.

There's always a problem here, he noted. The Bible never goes down easily among self-committed humans. The Bible is counter-cultural. It speaks *to* the culture, often even *against* the culture. If we're going to make a point from Scripture, it's going to be radical. It's almost axiomatic that the listener's natural explanation will conflict with the textual explanation of how things are, and how they ought to be. Jack could foresee a significant amount of struggle over this point in the process. If we really want this to work well, he reminded himself, we're going to have to help the listener overcome his or her objection to the text. He wrote the words, "What's the problem?" in quadrant three.

Finally, Jack noticed, quadrant four is about the connection between experience and today. This is where the Goodyears hit the pavement. If the message is to be persuasive, and not simply informative, then the intent has to include some kind of practical response or change on the part of those who attend the presentation. If there isn't any real change anticipated by the message, then why would we bother with the whole painful process? "What's the difference?" Jack wrote into the final space in quadrant four.

### Discovery Questions

- ▶ What's the story?
- ▶ What's the point?
- ▶ What's the problem?
- ▶ What's the difference?

He stopped to consider his work. That'll preach, he thought to himself, his enthusiasm mounting. I can do something with this! Jack picked up his stack of yellow sheets and decided to reconfigure his exegetical data so that they could serve as answers to these four key questions. It was a promising idea. Jack thought he remembered a comment from homiletics class, years before, that a preacher should do almost as much exegesis on the listeners as he does on the text. These four questions would make sure that he gave his listeners their due.

The integration inherent in the model also appealed to Jack. He liked the prospect of moving beyond the old three-points-and-a-poem approach. If he could give his listeners God's Word in a manner that respected them and dealt honestly with their concerns—integrating text, today, explanation, and experience—he might actually have a chance of helping contemporary people truly hear from God.

Jack glanced at the clock. Time was getting away from him, as usual, but he couldn't interrupt the process now. He had developed some helpful new ideas, but he hadn't even addressed his text yet.

---

*I [am rejoicing] in what was suffered for you, and I fill up in my flesh what is still lacking in regard to Christ's afflictions, for the sake of his body, which is the church. I have become its servant by the commission God gave me to present to you the word of God in its fullness—the mystery that has been kept hidden for ages and generations, but is now disclosed to the saints. To them God has chosen to make known among the Gentiles the glorious riches of this mystery, which is Christ in you, the hope of glory. We proclaim him, admonishing and teaching everyone with all wisdom, so that we may present everyone perfect in Christ. To this end I labor, struggling with all his energy, which so powerfully works in me.*

THE APOSTLE PAUL, COLOSSIANS 1:24–29 NIV.

So what about the Colossians text? Jack went right to work, beginning with quadrant one: "What's the story?" Rummaging through his notes, he began to look for clues, anything that would give him a sense of the story behind the propositions. It wouldn't be easy in a didactic text like this, but there had to be indicators. There had to be something he could use to help his listeners connect with the original issues in the original setting.

------------------

*The mystery of one's relationship to God cannot be cap-*
*tured in propositional form and passed directly from one*
*human being to another—not even if the sermon is im-*
*peccably logical and flawlessly delivered. It must be*
*wrapped, like faith itself, in the paradoxical distance and*
*intimacy that stories provide, in the grandeur of myth,*
*the lilt of songs, the memory of legend, and the seductive*
*disorientation of parables.*

ROBIN R. MEYERS, *WITH EARS TO HEAR*, 2–3.


Okay, Jack rubbed his temples, I'm looking for story elements—
human stuff. Colossae was a real city. There were real people in this
text. Paul himself, for instance. Paul wasn't personally acquainted with
the church at Colossae. The ministry in Colossae had begun as a kind
of daughter work of the Ephesian church through the ministry of
people like Epaphras and Philemon. So, this was Paul's opportunity
to share some of his passion and firm up the foundation that had been
established among these new believers.

That would be important in this case. Colossae was a city full of
religious options. With the philosophy sects, the mystery cults, the
Jewish influence, and the general Gnostic flavor to the city, the gospel would have to be clearly articulated in order to avoid getting swal-
lowed up by the cacophony of alternate voices and approaches.

People in Colossae had a long history of dealing with the age-old
mysteries: What does it mean to be spiritual? What is the ultimate
end of life? Who is God and what does he expect? The city overflowed
with possible answers to mysterious questions. People were coming
to Christ, but they didn't necessarily want to let go of their old answers and practices either. The tendency was to introduce ideas from
other philosophies and religions and incorporate them into their new
Christian worldview. Not unlike many Christians today, Jack noted.

The text raised some big, old questions about the nature of God,
the plan of God, and the openness of God. Old questions that were

anything but stale. Jack allowed himself a spreading smile. These old questions are the same questions raised by our culture here, today. These are questions that intrigue people, frighten people, comfort people, and vex people. It wasn't a narrative text with a discernible plotline, and yet there *was* a story here—a contemporary story. It was as if Colossae were a city just down the interstate.

So, "What's the point?" Jack picked up the yellow legal pad and moved to the couch he kept for visitors. Changing position might help him change the direction of his thinking as he approached the second quadrant. What's the key propositional concept intended by this text in Scripture? What's the big idea?

---

### *What's the Big Idea?*

HADDON W. ROBINSON, *BIBLICAL PREACHING*, 31.

Jack was able to detect several ideas at work in the text. There was Paul's willingness to suffer for the sake of the gospel. There was the challenge to proclaim the gospel, the mighty struggle to present everyone perfect in Christ. There was the intriguing question of how the energy of Christ worked powerfully within the one who preaches the gospel. One of the more significant emphases appeared to be the opening of the gospel to the Gentiles.

Yet, there was one message that seemed to transcend and summarize all of the others. It was an exciting idea that eerily echoed Jack's conversation with Henry from the day before. It was the idea of a mystery solved, of hidden things being laid open, of the revelation of things long misunderstood and obscured. It was the idea that God was revealing what had been kept hidden for ages and generations. All the clutter and corrosion that had confused people and kept them from knowing their creator was now being stripped back, peeled away, and laid open. God was solving the mystery by means of his Son, bringing hope and glory to people. Now, we can know the mystery of the ages, the truth about God, not because of our own wisdom or exalted good sense, but simply because God has made himself known to us—Christ in you, the hope of glory.

There was no fatigue now. Jack was fully focused, as he moved to consider the third quadrant of his model: "What's the problem?" Jack was stumped for a moment. What could possibly be the problem with a message so important, so potent? What possible objection could people have to a message . . . ?

Jack stopped himself. He was thinking like a preacher. He had to devote some of his time to thinking like the listener. It shouldn't be too hard, he told himself. He *was* a listener, the first listener, perhaps, but a listener just the same. As a fallen, finite human being, he only had to examine his own heart to determine the difficulty with the message the text was proposing.

The message was demanding, of course. If the mystery really was resolved in Jesus, the implication is that we would have to take Jesus seriously, believing in what he said and doing what he expected. It kind of takes the fun out of things. Isn't a mysterious God more interesting? Why do we have to solve the mystery? Why do we have to figure him out, lock it all down, and turn it into a major world religion? Couldn't we be content to leave God the way he is? Isn't he more appealing to us if we let the element of mystery alone?

---

*There are subjectivist epistemologies that belittle propositional revelation. There are linguistic theories that cultivate an exegetical atmosphere of ambiguity. There is a kind of popular, cultural relativism that enables people to dispense flippantly with uncomfortable biblical teaching. Where these kind of things take root, the Bible will be silenced in the church, and preaching will become a reflection of current issues and religious opinions.*

JOHN PIPER, *THE SUPREMACY OF GOD IN PREACHING*, 40.

Postmodern people love mystery. Solving mysteries smacks of over-confidence, though. Acknowledging and even celebrating mystery is a more honest, more pragmatic, and more openhearted approach. Jack remembered reading a theologian who suggested that the classic, modern approach to the mystery novel was Sherlock Holmes, who was able to come to a declarative sense of the truth through a simple, though sometimes painstaking, investigative process. The mystery was always solved, and everything was always left neat and tidy. A postmodern approach to the mystery novel might be John le Carré, the book said. Le Carré novels are more moody and open-ended. These stories are less about the facts and more about the ambiguity of truth, life, and morality. So why solve the mystery? Why reduce things to Jesus? Do we really expect people who are so fundamentally suspicious of easy answers to buy into a single solution? By accepting Jesus, don't I reject everyone else? Isn't that how it works? Is that what I really want? Isn't this a problem for us?

He had to stop. At least for a moment, he had to get up and move around. He had to think. It was the typical postmodern exit. People have lost confidence in their ability to choose. They're looking for a way to avoid responsibility. If everybody's right then nobody's wrong. The stakes are lowered, and people can simply fend for themselves.

---

*Everyone must look out for himself, and the best time is had by those who're best able to deceive themselves.*

FYODOR DOSTOYEVSKY, *CRIME AND PUNISHMENT*, 555.

And yet, was this any way to live? Where is the hope in this? Where is the future? Jack could feel it in his marrow—a building sense of courage that might, in fact, give him the ability actually to preach. He could contend for truth. He could offer hope and a future. It was right there in the text: the hope of glory.

That's my quadrant four. He surprised himself with the thought.

"What's the difference?" Jesus is the difference. The beauty of the mystery of the gospel is that it is Christ *in* us. God reveals himself personally, literally taking up residence in our heart and lives. It is Christ in us that gives us hope, and hope makes the fundamental difference. Hope brings joy, meaning, and possibilities, overturning postmodern cynicism and offering a reason to get out of bed in the morning. Hope brings *life*.

Wow! Pastor Jack Newman was stunned momentarily. It was still a little rough, but he had the makings of something preachable. He had a message. From here, the step to the second stage, sermon construction, would not be all that large. For the first time in a while, Jack could feel anticipation building for Sunday morning, and this time it was a good feeling.

——————

In the sanctuary, the pulpit stood in darkened dormancy, patiently waiting for a congregation, a preacher, and a sermon. Jack Newman's moment would come.

# 4

# Second Stage: Construction
## THE SERMON

Sam Sidhu didn't like mornings. It was just that there didn't seem to be any other time to do these things. Pastors are always talking about how people need to sacrifice their time in the Lord's service, he mused, but then they want to clock out after their forty hours. I put in fifty to sixty hours a week, and then I have to do the church accounts on top of it all. It was a familiar whine.

The church's volunteer treasurer poured himself a cup of strong coffee and brought the battered file box to the kitchen table. Of course, first he had to clear the table of the evening dishes, newspapers, toys, and crumbs left over from someone's late-night snack. He really should have an office at home, he reminded himself. Yet, with five family members sharing three bedrooms as it was, finding room for even a desk and a computer was difficult.

He took out the teller's sheet from the previous Sunday. The job was easier, he admitted, when there was enough money, and there had been money lately, thanks to an anonymous giver. Sam was the one person in the church who knew who gave what. It was a burden he would rather not have borne, but there was nothing he could do about it. Someone had to be able to issue tax receipts. It was a sacred trust, hard to maintain at church business meetings when certain members had more to say than what their giving patterns might deem appropriate. But Sam was an honorable man. He knew how to keep his mouth shut.

But this one was hard to figure. Digging into the file box, he retrieved the records of the previous six months' offerings. There it was. Three separate donations of five thousand dollars each, given in cash at irregular intervals. There may have been more of them if he were to dig a little further back. Each time, the money had come in a plain, white envelope, which meant that there was no donation number and no way to determine who had given the money. This was highly unusual. The church tellers had felt a little uneasy handling that much cash. Whoever had been giving this money was entitled to a significant tax deduction. If they don't want the money, Sam thought to himself, they should claim it anyway, and then they could give the tax refund too. In truth, it was none of his business, but it was so unusual . . .

Sam Sidhu took a long sip of coffee. It wasn't hot enough. He put the cup in the microwave and punched the buttons. Hearing the familiar whirring sound, he picked up the phone and began to dial. Then again, it was probably too early. He would call later in the day.

---

Jack Newman returned to work early Thursday morning so he could get a good start on his sermon. He'd been sufficiently encouraged the day before to warrant another day at it. He switched on the computer and stared at the screen. The state-of-the-art laptop was new to him. He'd been able to get in on a company deal through the good graces of one of the guys on the church board. Now, he was starting to wonder whether it was such a great thing. The computer would eventually make his life a little easier, if he could ever manage to get the thing configured. Jack had used a Macintosh for years and still used an older one at home. But this Windows platform was a whole different world.

The computer was one thing, but then a guy had to decipher the software too. A true Mac loyalist, Jack was not impressed by the experience. Still, he thought, I'm a reasonably intelligent person. I should be able to figure this out.

There were a couple of e-mail messages waiting in his inbox. Junk mail as usual, of course. How he got onto these lists he had no idea. There was also a message from Kevin, a friend of Jack's from seminary. Kevin was a collector of Internet humor, and Jack had been added to his list. I wonder who writes this stuff, and where in the world it comes from? The question was referred to no one in particular. He called up the message, which was directed personally to him:

To: PastorJack@pulpitserve.com
From: KevJ@direx.ca
Subject: this one's just for you
Hey Jack. I know how discouraged you've been trying to figure out your new computer and software. You like oxymorons? Let me brighten your day with a new one I just heard: MICROSOFT WORKS.

Jack laughed out loud, though it was probably more of a snort than a true laugh. The joke wasn't hilarious, but it did truthfully represent his current opinion of the product. Oxymorons were like that. Perfectly normal words until someone points out the incongruity. Jumbo Shrimp. Military Intelligence. Airline food. There were a million of them.

### Oxymorons

- ▶ act naturally
- ▶ alone together
- ▶ bad health
- ▶ found missing
- ▶ freezer burn
- ▶ good grief
- ▶ legally drunk
- ▶ literal interpretation

▶ original copy
▶ political science
▶ small crowd
▶ soft rock
▶ sweet sorrow
▶ taped live
▶ work party

There are oxymorons in the Bible, Jack realized. The thought surprised him. Grace and truth; Word and flesh; sovereignty and free will; in the world yet not of the world; in each case, the Bible unites competing concepts in ways that both surprise and help us.

Jack thought of his preaching and coined a few more: narrative explanation; ancient relevance; expository encounter . . .

—⁓⟨⟩⁓—

Tom Newman arrived at city hall before the doors were opened. They should give me a key to the place, he thought. He was certainly there often enough. The building could use a cleaning, he decided, as he peered through the glass doors. It was a wonderful example of art deco architecture. It could have been stylish if it hadn't been buried under so much grime and dust. A new carpet wouldn't hurt either, he noticed.

Tom checked his watch. It would be another five minutes before the camera crew would arrive. Who knows when security would actually open the building. They had to be there early to get set up before the mayor's arrival. He decided he wanted to get this thing done early so it could be presented live on the local morning shows.

Tom still wasn't sure where the interview was going to go, but he wasn't in the habit of denying the mayor exposure. There was usually a modest ratings boost involved.

—⁓⟨⟩⁓—

Stephen Lang poured corn flakes into his bowl then went to the fridge for a jug of milk. Except there *was* no jug of milk. The environmentalist knew he should have stopped on the way home from the office the day before. He'd even written himself a note, "Get milk!" and had stuck it to the fridge underneath the "Fritz Friesen Sells Homes" magnet. This showed he'd been alert, but just not alert enough to be helpful. A wise man would have put the note in his pocket or written it on the back of his hand or done something to remind himself, just so he wouldn't have to eat dry corn flakes this morning—again!

He turned his attention to the kitchen television and turned the sound up when he saw the mayor. His Worship is up early this morning, Lang noticed, and looking fine as usual. That man knew how to smile, that was for sure.

---

This was probably a mistake, Tom told himself. That's what he told himself every time he interviewed Sims. The guy was so good with his hundred-watt smile and his "I care" persona. Tom always felt that he was being manipulated, that the mayor was using him to advance his agenda. Of course, from Sims's perspective, that's exactly what he was doing, Tom reminded himself. He was Sims's access to the city. Most reporters, however, weren't used to thinking of themselves strictly as go-betweens.

"This is a great city," Theodore Sims beamed. The mayor was firmly in control. Tom knew he had to be careful. Somehow, he wanted to steer the agenda without making it look as if he was trying to manipulate the interview. "I don't know when we've been in better shape," Sims continued. "We're seeing new businesses start and old businesses renewed. We're a city full of talented, confident people who know what they want and how to get there. At city hall we're just trying to get out of the way. The goal of our administration is to eliminate obstacles and create an environment in which the talented people of our city can prosper. Economic indicators . . ."

"But it's not all so positive," Tom interrupted clumsily. He didn't want the interview to turn into an early campaign speech.

"Tom, I'm surprised at you." Sims didn't miss a trick. "You're not one of those naysayers, are you?"

"Sure, business is growing," Tom pushed on, "but what about those who say that a certain amount of restriction is important in order to protect quality of life?"

"Here, I thought you were a member of the impartial media. You haven't got a membership card for the other party tucked away in your wallet, do you?" Sims had a way of chiding you with a twinkle in his eye, leaving observers with the impression that it was just good-natured ribbing. But the point was made.

Tom took the bait, "No sir, you know me better than that. I have no agenda, and I resent you suggesting that I do. I just feel it's important to raise the questions people are asking. There are a lot of people out there who would suggest you've been excessively optimistic." Too far, Tom rebuked himself. Way too far. He couldn't believe how this guy always made him feel like an amateur, as if he were the interview subject.

"Mayor Pollyanna," Sims laughed warmly. "Is that it?" The mayor looked directly into the camera, ignoring Tom Newman altogether. "I understand that my critics are trying to paint me as an out-of-control business lackey. I'm supposed to be an evil power broker who won't rest until every field is paved, every pond is drained, with condos on every hill and strip malls on every corner. I'm a very frightening person, apparently. Look," Sims leaned forward, "taxes are down, unemployment is down, consumer spending is up, we're opening two new parks on the east side this month as well as a new ice arena in Hollowfield, just in time for the winter season. You've got more money in your pockets. Maybe your old mayor's not doing such a bad job after all."

Tom signed off lamely. Not the brightest moment in his journalistic career.

---

"That should take some pressure off," the president of Dogwood Developments allowed, as he switched off the television. People wouldn't be fooled by the performance, but they would be distracted for a while. Sims's college football career was coming in handy. It never hurt to have the mayor blocking for you.

Jack Newman waited impatiently as the familiar computer dial tone crackled from his modem. It was ironic how computers, which were supposed to speed up your life, seemed to involve so much waiting.

## www.preaching.org

A forum for the discussion of the practice of preaching, the shape of culture, and the points of connection between the two.

The familiar welcome screen came up, and Jack went to his bookmark section. Somewhere in here he had marked a preaching site . . . there, www.preaching.org.

The site loaded quickly, and Jack scrolled down the list of feature articles. There were plenty of places on the Internet to find sermon outlines and illustrations but not many places like this one, where you were encouraged to critically consider the task of preaching itself.

Jack had noticed an article a few weeks earlier that he thought might be able to help him as he actually got down to constructing his sermon. He found it quickly: "An Integrative Model for Preaching." The author was working with a model similar to the one Jack had already worked out for himself, suggesting that the incarnation of Jesus Christ, Word become flesh, was a fitting model for the kind of integration necessary in preaching. Integration, Jack smiled. Maybe his thinking wasn't as unique as he'd thought.

---

*The incarnation, therefore, is the truest theological model for preaching because it was God's ultimate act of communication. Jesus, who was the Christ, most perfectly said God to us because the eternal Word took on human flesh in a contemporary situation. Preaching cannot do otherwise.*

CLYDE E. FANT, *PREACHING FOR TODAY*, 70.

Jack found a piece of scrap paper. He fiddled with his mechanical pencil for a moment. He could never load a new piece of lead without breaking two or three of them off. Once he had his pencil in order, Jack began to sketch out his model; explanation over experience, text beside today. What's the story, what's the point, what's the problem, what's the difference, he reminded himself. He liked the symmetry of the four questions. They had helped him discover the message he wanted to communicate, but he still didn't really have a sermon. He had a lot of data, but he didn't yet know how he was going to communicate it to the people.

The Web-site article suggested that sermon building requires the preacher to make choices, a great many choices, to create a vehicle that will drive the message into the consciousness, belief, and behavior of the listener. Words must be chosen. Images, concepts, and metaphors have to be considered, selected, and employed so that they give

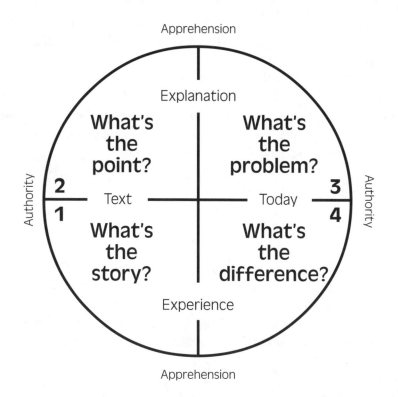

the listener the best possible opportunity to hear from God and respond appropriately. The choices are both substantive and structural. Substantive choices have to do with the concepts that will be presented, the shape or flow of the sermonic section, and the emotional pull. Structural choices involve the crafting of theme statements, tag lines, and a compelling title for the sermon.

Jack heard a car pull up in the parking lot outside his window. He got up and closed the office door so that he wouldn't be distracted. It was most likely someone from the Young Moms group, setting up for the meeting later on. Ordinarily Jack would have gotten up to say hello. Always good to show one's face. Not today, he thought. He was focused on his reading.

When making substantive choices in the building of the sermon, the preacher will need to consider ways to engage the listener as well as ways to teach him or her. The preacher will need to be honest, convincing, and motivating, and he will have to get the point across quickly. Contemporary listeners come equipped with a remote-control channel changer in their heads. It takes most people split seconds to determine whether to stick with a particular television channel. The preacher has little more than that to convince the listener to pay attention.

———

*The first three minutes before an audience determines whether or not they will hear us at all. . . . If their attention is not snagged in the first three minutes of a presentation, it will be nearly impossible to gain it back.*

CALVIN MILLER, *THE EMPOWERED COMMUNICATOR*, 19.

The article suggested specific ways to think about the substance of the sermon. Surprisingly, the four suggested categories were remarkably compatible with the model that Jack had been constructing for himself. "So what?" was the author's first concern. Jack put it in quadrant one. He was familiar with the question. Lots of books on preaching suggested it, but normally this kind of question was asked at the end of the sermon, as a way of ensuring that there was a relevant application to the message. Dealing with the "So what?" concern at the beginning of the sermon was new to Jack. It made some sense, however. Maybe preachers used to be able to assume their listeners understood why they should attend to the sermon, but that assumption was no longer safe. Nobody comes to my church anxious to receive the pearls of truth and wisdom that drop from my lips, Jack smiled. Safer to assume that they'll be preoccupied and even a little antagonistic. "Show me why I should invest myself in this thing!" In other words, expect the listeners to greet you with a great big "So what?"

Putting the "So what?" issue into the first quadrant created an interesting dynamic, Jack noticed. Normally, I would answer the "So what?" with logical argument, he thought. But he had enough pulpit experience to know that logical introductions seldom created much in the way of interest. The model he was working with began with the experience of the text. In his first stage, the struggle to discover the message in the text, he had begun with the biblical story. It's hard to beat human interest as a way of gaining attention right off the top, he reminded himself.

But this is not what the textbooks advise, at least the older ones. Jack remembered being advised that the way to bridge the gap between the ancient text and the contemporary situation was to "principlize" the text. The challenge was to find propositions that transcend the specific cultural situation and bring those to bear on the listener. The "timeless truth", then, became the point of connection for the listener.

Jack had never been entirely happy about this approach, however, for a couple of reasons. First of all, postmoderns have never found propositions all that friendly, and second, most biblical propositions were particularly prickly. Jack recalled his sermon from a few weeks earlier on Genesis 22—Abraham and Isaac on Mt. Moriah. What is the timeless truth from that passage? Trust God no matter what. Believe that he knows what he's doing even if he requires from you the life of your only son. Now *there's* a user-friendly proposition, Jack chuckled at the thought.

---

*Preaching does not stop with understanding ancient languages, history, culture, and customs. Unless the centuries can be bridged with contemporary relevance in the message, then the preaching experience differs little from a classroom encounter. One must first process the text for original meaning and then principlize the text for current applicability. One's study falls short of the goal if this step is omitted or slighted.*

RICHARD L. MAYHUE, "REDISCOVERING
EXPOSITORY PREACHING," 16.

The problem is that biblical propositions are always "in your face." They challenge us by their very definition. They're not warm and fuzzy, like in the case when Jesus called the disciples to take up their cross. They wouldn't have heard that one the way that we do, Jack knew. They didn't put crosses in front of their churches and hang mini-crosses around their necks. That would be like our setting up electric chairs on sanctuary platforms. Crucifixion was the most brutal form of capital punishment known to people at the time. The disciples must have really choked to hear Jesus say this.

---

*The distance between ourselves and the original readers of the text is in a measure bridged by our common humanity.*

FRED CRADDOCK, *PREACHING*, 134.

Propositions have to be made, but they probably aren't the best place to start. If the task is to connect the listeners with the text and engage them with the sermon, it might be better to think in terms of the people rather than the principles. How, then, do you answer the

"So what?" question? By engaging the listeners' human qualities, speaking to their hearts, making them feel things, locating them in the story of the text so that they can actually identify with the real human beings that constitute the Bible. Remember those Colossians, Jack reminded himself. They really existed, and they're probably not so different from the people I'm preaching to every Sunday. If I can help my listeners connect and commiserate with the people in the Bible, they'll have a reason to attend to the propositions when we get to them.

Jack found that the author's second point fit well in quadrant two: "What's what?" It's a lot easier to answer the question "What's what?" when you've already helped the listeners buy into the "So what?" Listeners who are emotionally engaged in a message will be ready to hear the propositions of the message even if they're confrontational.

Jack considered several of the texts that he had recently preached. Some of the texts, like many of those from his series in Romans, required a great amount of detailed explanation of the text. Working in this quadrant would, then, require quite a bit more time. On the other hand, narrative or poetic passages might not require much explanation at all. If the preacher has told a parable so well that the listeners are emotionally involved in the presentation, then there might not be a whole lot left to say in quadrant two. A forthright statement of the point might be all it takes. When you've told a story well, the punch line can have a lot of power. It doesn't always need embellishing.

———

*A very little exegesis is enough for the average sermon and in an expository sermon one is in constant temptation to make burdensome the exegetical explanations. To know how to give just enough and not too much exegesis is a harder task than the making of another kind of sermon.*

T. P. STAFFORD, "EXPOSITORY PREACHING: A CRITICISM," 232.

This is probably where I've spent most of my time in the sermons I've preached, Jack realized. I've always felt a need to overexplain. Maybe I wanted people to believe I was a deep thinker, or maybe I felt a need to share every little thing that I'd picked up in my study, or maybe I just didn't know any other way. The thing is, not everything you read in a commentary has to be worked into the sermon.

On the other hand, people aren't stupid either. The message has to make sense to them if I expect them to apprehend it. No pendulum swinging, Jack reminded himself. Just because traditional preaching has been *so* dependant upon the mind doesn't mean that I should be avoiding it or giving it the short shrift. Integration with integrity demands that I fully satisfy the cognitive needs of the listeners. According to the web article, the communicator has to influence the cognitive (head), and the affective (heart), in order to get at the behavioral (hands). If everything I do is on the affective level, telling stories and creating environments that play with the listener's emotions, I may be able to create certain desirable behavioral changes, but there won't likely be much depth or substance to them. The mind matters. I can't let myself think purely in terms of holding attention, being clever or gripping. It's actually important that I have something to say and that I say it with intellectual credibility. People want to know "What's what?"

---

*Cognitive (head) + Affective (heart) = Behavioral (hands)*

The office was unusually quiet. Jack had looked into getting one of those cable connections to the Internet so that he wouldn't tie up his telephone while he was doing research on the web. Come to think of it, there were advantages to having the phone line effectively tied up. The pastor stood up for a minute and raised his hands to the air. He locked his fingers together as if to pray then extended them upward, palms to the ceiling, pressing hard. Slowly, he rotated his neck around from side to side. Sighing deeply, he let his hands down and returned to the article.

"So what?" and "What's what?" The third stage was "Yeah, but . . ."
This is where the argument starts. This is where things get interesting. "*Yeah*, I understand the point," the listener says, "*but* I'm thinking something different." "*Yeah*, I know what it is you're saying, *but*
actually I've always looked at it this way. . . ." Jack wrote the words,
"Yeah, but . . ." into the third quadrant of his model at the intersec-
tion of explanation and today.

---

*The problem of pre-understanding, however, does not give
grounds for the cynical response that the modern interpreter understands the Bible only on the basis of his own
presuppositions. For there is an ongoing process of dialogue with the text in which the text itself progressively
corrects and reshapes the interpreter's own questions and
assumptions.*

ANTHONY C. THISELTON, *THE TWO HORIZONS*, 439.

Whenever you offer a point on the basis of objective authority, you
can expect that there will be cognitive dissonance for subjective listeners. Listeners bring all their assumptions and presuppositions to
the party. These presets will not be easily overturned just because
some independent authority tells them so. Listeners will always sift
what they hear according to what they already understand to be true.
The communicator, on the other hand, is trying to change the listeners' minds so that they will buy the communicator's argument or deter-
gent. But people don't change "brands" without a struggle, especially
when it comes to biblical concepts.

Jack was thinking about those hard statements in the Bible again.
If people are cognitively conditioned to think that self-satisfaction is
the primary concern, the biblical presentation of selflessness is not
going to be easily assimilated. In fact, the whole purpose of the Bible
is to challenge the convictions and presuppositions of the contempo-

rary mind. There is always going to be a "Yeah, but . . ." when we're talking about the Bible, Jack realized. The listener has to be convinced.

He pondered the model he'd been sketching for a moment. He drew a broad circle around the four quadrants. It looked a little like a target now, or like the tachometer on his car dashboard. If the needle started at the bottom of the dial, it would sweep the left-hand side without much difficulty. But at the top of the screen it would face some resistance moving into the right-hand side. That needle would start to quiver and shake. The objective is moving into enemy territory. The subjective will not easily want to be objectified. The listener will not easily want to be won.

And yet, Jack thought, this aspect of preaching could be so productive. Everybody's got a problem with the Bible, if we're being honest. We're all so selfish that the Bible always comes as a challenge to us, if we're paying attention. So, why not take advantage of it? What a great way to hold attention and engage listeners on a deeper level, to get

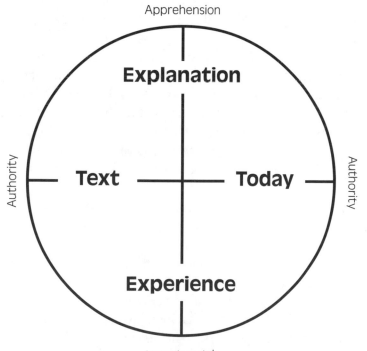

under the listeners' skin! Listeners have their objections. Why not surface them and work with them?

### Construction Concerns

- ▶ So what?
- ▶ What's what?
- ▶ Yeah, but . . .
- ▶ Now what?

Yet, most preachers don't want to go this far, he realized. I never have. The thought challenged him. My tendency has been to make my point and then to sit down as if the listeners would buy into it purely on my say-so. That's probably not realistic, he reminded himself. Even if listeners did buy the idea on purely objective grounds, the conviction might not run very deep unless the preacher can find a way to challenge their original preconceptions. Minds don't change without a fight, the article said. Fur will fly! Could make for exciting preaching!

Jack noticed the clock in the corner. It always ran five minutes fast or five minutes slow. For some reason, he couldn't remember which it was just at the moment. Either way, he realized he still hadn't actually done any work on his sermon. All in good time, he told himself. He was learning something. He focused on the computer screen again. The author had one more issue to address.

"Now what?" It was a good question. Jack wrote the two words into the final quadrant in his model where today (the subjective) intersected with experience (intuition). A perfect fit. At the end of the day, the listeners need not only to think differently but also to feel differently and ultimately to act differently. Once the communicator overcomes the listeners' cognitive objections, there's still the matter of action. The mind counts for a lot, but the mind isn't the whole.

Jack thought about all the effort preachers put into changing listeners' minds. So, why are the behavioral results so pathetic? The polls say we've got all these people who believe in God and are committed to Christian principles. Why, then, do we see so little change in the practical life and morality of the nation? Maybe because a change of mind is not enough, Jack reflected.

Could be, he thought. I certainly believe more than I act on. Just because I change my mind doesn't necessarily mean that I'm going to change my will. I can believe something intellectually, but in order for it to alter my behavior it's going to have to touch me at a deeper level.

Jack thought about his father, a long-time cigarette smoker. He recalled the frustrating arguments he used to have with his dad. Didn't he know that cigarettes were eventually going to kill him? Didn't he trust the scientists who talked about how harmful smoking was to health? Of course, he knew. He just didn't seem to care. Why do you do it? Jack used to ask. Don't you understand what it will do to you? Don't you believe the surgeon general?

No, his father would respond, I understand this will probably kill me. It probably won't be pretty, either.

So why do you do it? Jack would ask in exasperation.

Because I like it, came the response. It's a habit. It makes me feel comfortable. It's just what I do.

None of those reasons have anything to do with cognition, Jack realized. The smoker's mind is convinced, but his will is not yet affected sufficiently to influence real behavioral change.

So how do I help the listener *want* to change? Jack wondered. What can I do to create an environment where the listener not only knows what to do but also is motivated to act on that knowledge?

That's where the emotion and experience have a place, the article said. A communicator can tell stories, paint pictures, and be emotive. Who hasn't been moved by hearing a great piece of music or a powerful work of drama? If the response is purely emotional, it'll not go very far, but if coupled with the appropriate cognitive conviction, something powerful could happen. If a listener not only knows what must be done but also actually feels like doing it, the communicator can bring about real change. Subject the whole process to the power of the Holy Spirit, Jack thought, and something dynamic will happen.

———

*What is needed today then is the same synthesis of reason and emotion, exposition and exhortation, as was achieved by Paul.*

JOHN R. W. STOTT, *BETWEEN TWO WORLDS*, 283.

"So what?" "What's what?" "Yeah but . . ." and "Now what?" It's in moving all the way around the circle that the message has power. The challenge, then, is to fill in the sermon with concepts and examples, images and metaphors. According to the article, there is more to enlivening sermons than going to the *5,000 Sermon Illustrations* volume that had been collecting dust on Jack's shelf for several years.

He took a deep breath and gazed at the ceiling for several moments before he logged off the Internet connection. Ideas were popping as he began to think specifically of the Colossians text he would be preaching this Sunday. This could be *fun*, he smiled.

———

Conrad Liu was ensconced in his cubicle. One of these days, he would have a real office, maybe even downtown in the new police headquarters building they were planning to build next year. It was hard to concentrate sometimes, when all you had were three flimsy walls that only went halfway to the ceiling. On the other hand, at least he was still out on the floor in the middle of things. It could occasionally be exciting.

But not today. This was grunt work. Pouring over telephone records would not fit anyone's definition of a good time, the detective was quite sure. This was due process. The politics of the thing was a little overheated, so he had to cross his i's and dot his t's, or the other way around. He was covering his tail like all good civic employees had been sworn to do since the beginning of time. It was all about *optics*. Making sure he was *seen* to have fulfilled all righteousness. Assuming, of course, that his assumption was right. Of course these boys had acted alone. The politicians were just sniping at each other like they always did. It was opportunism, he was sure.

Then, again . . . the suspects had a cell phone. Liu was reviewing the records. The calls seemed mostly routine. The only number that dominated belonged to the older suspect's girlfriend. There wasn't much activity on Sunday, he noticed. What time was the crime? Had to have been after nine and before ten. Witnesses had seen the suspects at the KFC at nine in the evening and the pastor had spotted them, or people that looked like them, from his office window around ten. There was only one phone call made on Sunday night, and that was at five past ten. Conrad studied the number. Why did it look familiar to him? He closed his eyes, folded his hands behind his head and did a slow spin in his swivel chair. Where had he seen that number?

Tom Newman pressed the final number into the keypad and waited for the city councilman to answer. Philip Andrews picked up on the first ring. Ya' gotta love cell phones, Newman smiled. No secretaries to get in the way. You just reach out and touch someone. "Did you happen to see the mayor's interview this morning?" he opened. "The mayor was quite convincing."

"Not one of your better interviews, Tom," Andrews chided. "I'm counting on you to hold the man's feet to the fire."

There was an edge to the councilman's voice. Tom found himself feeling defensive. "I'm not on your payroll, Mr. Andrews. I just provide the opportunity for the man's voice to be heard—just like I'm doing for you right now. If anybody's going to hold someone's feet to the fire, I'd have thought it was your job."

"Look, Newman, I know what happened, and I know what the mayor did, but I can't go on the record with that kind of stuff. My lawyers wouldn't be amused."

"It appears you know more than most, sir. But let me ask you something else, then. I've been noticing some inconsistencies between your voting record and your public comments. Do you care to comment about . . . ?"

"My record speaks for itself," Andrews interrupted.

"So do your public statements," Newman countered. "You've been forcefully arguing for environmental sensitivity, which is hard to justify given that you haven't actually voted in support of an environmental initiative since you were elected."

"Since when do my public comments have to be consistent with my voting record? What does one have to do with the other?"

"Sir?"

"This is politics, my friend. If you don't know how the game is played by now . . ." Andrews' voice faded.

Tom Newman held the phone to his ear long after the councilman's phone had disconnected. The reporter wasn't used to such candor from the smooth-talking politician. Had he just been played? Or . . .

Pastor Jack was ready to get down to business. He had a message, "Christ in you is the mystery solved." Now he needed a framework sufficient to communicate the message. He needed the words and the approach that would enable him to bring about change in the listener's experience. He needed a sermon.

Specifically, Jack reminded himself, he needed a title, and some strong tag lines would help, too. If he was going to work his way around the four quadrants of his new model, it would help if he had a few strong phrases that would give some direction to his thinking. His plan was to signpost the movement of the sermon by means of simple mnemonic phrases that could stick in people's minds without being as obvious as traditional point statements tended to be.

------

*It must embody the biblical understanding that the cognitive dimension does not exhaust either the human person, reality as a whole, or the truth of God. . . . Rather, our theology must give place to the concept of "mystery"—not as an irrational aspect alongside the rational, but as a reminder of the fundamentally nonrational or suprarational reality of God.*

STANLEY J. GRENZ, "STAR TREK AND THE NEXT GENERATION," 99.

First, he needed a strong image to work with. The best place to find an image, of course, is in the text itself. In this case, the word that kept leaping to the front in his consideration of his text, Colossians 1:24–29, was "mystery." There was a lot of mystery in this text. The mystery for the Colossian Gentiles was how to know and please God. They didn't have the kind of access to God that the Jews had, so they were mixing and matching various religious experiences and ideas, trying to find something that would work for them.

The mystery for Paul was a little different. Jack could imagine Paul wondering whether he was on the right track in this ministry to the Gentiles. He'd been raised to believe that his own people, Israel, were God's chosen nation. But now he was working both sides of the street, and that had made a lot of people very unhappy with him. So, what was God doing, anyway? Did the Jews have a proprietary interest in God? Was he right to be offering the gospel to the Gentiles?

The mystery for Jack himself and for his listeners was very personal. What did it mean to have Christ in you? he wondered. It was the whole postmodern problem, really. How does one experience the transcendent, objective God of the universe within the limitations of a personal, subjective human life? God is doing something big here, he realized. The concept of mystery would give Jack a rich source of imagery to play with in his presentation.

The title came to him quickly: "Unsolved Mysteries." It was stolen from the old television series, obviously, but that would give it just the right amount of cultural familiarity, and it would reflect the challenge of the text and the imagery of the sermon.

Now he needed to add the tag lines. The first one was easy: "Life is full of mystery." With a line like that, he could intersect the listeners' personal stories with the back-story to the Colossians text. The "So what?" is answered by our common experience of befuddlement. Everyone knows what it's like to be confused by mystery. Life is bigger than we are, and so are our questions.

The second tag surprised Jack when it came to him. "Jesus solves the mystery." It was clean, simple, and it was declarative. Jack had not expected to be able to unite the complexity of the text in such a succinct statement. The more he thought about it, however, the more he was convinced that he'd come up with an effective way of stating "What's what?" The mystery that had been hidden for ages and generations was now being revealed in Jesus. The point is that the deepest and most challenging questions known to humanity find their answer in the preaching of Jesus Christ who indwells us to make God known to us.

Jack had to ruminate a little before coming up with the third tag line. The second quadrant could come across as simplistic to many

# Unsolved Mysteries
## Colossians 1:24–29

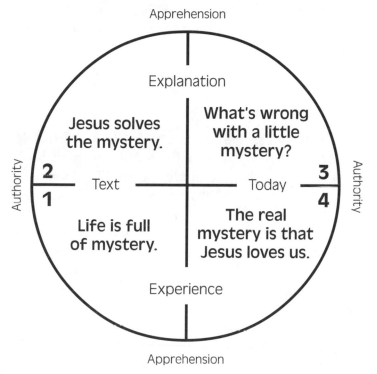

people. It was like the standard children's Sunday school answer to every question: Jesus. But for many listeners, the mystery would seem deeper and darker than that. "What's wrong with a little mystery?" Many of the listeners actually enjoy mystery, he realized. Besides, some would argue that this is the kind of mystery that defies solution. *Yeah,* I understand that Jesus came to reveal God to us, *but* doesn't that seem a little arrogant? Do we really want to say that somehow we've cornered the truth? Are we really all agreed that Jesus is the only possible way to access truth and everybody else with a different idea or a different pathway is mistaken, or worse?

———

*How is it possible to judge the worldview of another person or group of people to be wrong when we realize that we have no privileged, universal access to truth and so can only pass judgment from the perspective of our own worldview?*

J. RICHARD MIDDLETON AND BRIAN J. WALSH, *TRUTH IS STRANGER THAN IT USED TO BE*, 30.

Jack found himself feeling uncomfortable with this line of thought. It felt wrong somehow to say such things, but perhaps that was what made it a good thing for him to do. He knew good and well that these were the kinds of thoughts that lay hidden under the surface of the people's minds. It was a good "Yeah, but . . ." he decided. It was a good way to get underneath the superficial thoughts that lay limp on the surface. Of course, he wouldn't leave the listeners there. The challenge would be to see if he could move them from saying, "Yeah, but . . ." to saying, "Yeah, OK" If not, he chuckled, we'll all have to move back to Colossae.

For the final quadrant, Jack wanted to build confidence in Jesus while acknowledging the mystery inherent in the idea of "Christ in you." It was time to move to a more intuitive, emotive experience of the gospel. We have to engage the mystery even as we experience its solution in Jesus. This quadrant will be difficult, he realized. Somehow I have to bring closure and a sense of motivation to the people, while expanding their vision of a big, mysterious God.

"The real mystery is that Jesus loves us." He repeated it to himself softly, and he loved it. With this kind of tag line, Jack could turn the presentation toward the listener, maintain the greater sense of divine mystery, while still pointing to Jesus Christ and his love as the foundation for our hope. It was this sense of hope that Jack wanted to appeal to. This could be the element that would inspire the people to make a change in their lives.

"Life is full of mystery. Jesus solves the mystery. What's wrong with a little mystery? The real mystery is that Jesus loves us." Not bad,

Jack affirmed. There was the sermon in four simple sentences. Now all he had to do was fill things in.

He took a sip from the can of Pepsi that had been sitting on the window ledge behind his chair. He almost spit it out. Warm and flat! How long had it been sitting there, anyway? He gulped the rest of it down regardless. Caffeine was his ally.

Jack returned to his task with a renewed determination. He realized that he hadn't been caught up in a sermon like this for a long time. The phone didn't ring. No one knocked on the door. It was a minor miracle. Jack looked up from his work and checked the clock. Almost two hours had passed. He remembered his lunch appointment and panicked for a minute. A quick calculation told him he had just enough time to jump in the car and get across town. He'd make it, barely.

He allowed himself one last look at his work. He would enjoy preaching this. The mystery imagery pervaded the sermon, giving it a feeling of unity. He thought he could engage the listeners by narrating their own experience of mystery, connecting it with that of the Colossian believers.

Next, he would unravel the complexities of the text, explaining "What's what?" with regard to the mystery of the indwelling revelation of God in Christ. It was a heavy subject, but Jack thought he'd come up with a way to illustrate his point, that the person of Jesus solves the biggest mystery of all, that is: "What do I do with God?"

In the third quadrant, he would try to go a little deeper and get under the skin of his listeners. Undoubtedly, they would find the Jesus answer too simplistic. He could imagine them saying, *yeah,* Jesus is great, *but* you can't reduce God as easily as all that. He had learned enough about postmodernism this week to understand that his biggest problem would be to define Jesus enough to help his listeners connect with the truth about God—without turning him into a two-dimensional cardboard character.

Ultimately, he wanted his listeners to realize a fresh appreciation of the love of God expressed in Jesus. "The real mystery is that Jesus loves us." He would help them imagine living in the mystery of "Christ in you."

———————

*When confronted by the intricacies of real events as people actually experience them in time, our pat and precise definitions do not work. And most of us know all of this quite well in our usual rounds of ministry. But get us in the pulpit, and all of a sudden life turns simple, clear, and unambiguous!*

EUGENE L. LOWRY, *DOING TIME IN THE PULPIT*, 48.

Jack's mind was buzzing as he left the office for his appointment. His car radio had been left on from his drive into work, but he didn't even notice the talk show banter. His mind was on his message. He imagined himself behind the pulpit on Sunday morning. The image was attractive to him for a change.

———————

Fortunately, the door was unlocked. He was prepared to break in if he had to, but it was simpler this way. He dropped the envelope on the driver's seat then closed the door. The act was so ordinary, it was hard to appreciate the seriousness of what he'd done. Anyone watching wouldn't have noticed anything unusual about the man as he ambled across the broadcasters' employee parking lot, except perhaps the crooked little grin on Franklin Porter's face.

# 5

# Third Stage: Assimilation
## UNCTION

Tom Newman felt surprisingly fresh, considering it was so early in the morning. He checked for his keys before locking the door, grabbed his briefcase and cell phone, and made his way to the car. He hadn't thought he would sleep so well, given the way he was feeling the night before. It was long after dark when he'd finally wrapped things up at the office, and this hadn't pleased his wife. He had to make his own supper, which turned out to be a couple of microwaved hot dogs in stale whole-wheat buns. There was nothing worth watching on the television, except the eleven o'clock reruns of his dismal morning show interview with the mayor, so he hadn't retired in his normal, good humor. The morning brought sunshine, however, and, after all, it was Friday. He almost caught himself whistling on the way out to the car—almost.

He noticed some paper crumpled on his seat, half-stuffed into the crack between the seat back and the seat bottom. It looked as if he'd been sitting on it. Maybe he hadn't noticed it in the dark.

He examined the envelope briefly before opening it. It looked a little mysterious. There was no return address and no markings except his initials in penciled, block letters. He tore the envelope open and leaned back against the garage wall. "Good morning, Mr. Andrews!" Tom said it out loud as he examined the contents of the envelope. It was a photocopy of the donations declaration for city counselor, Philip Andrews. Such declarations were not unusual. Every local politician was required by law to declare all major campaign donations they'd received above a thousand dollars. These donations were a matter of public record. Freedom of information statutes demanded their availability to the media and to the public at large. It was just that no one ordinarily paid any attention to them. Clearly, someone intended Tom Newman to pay attention to this list.

The photocopy was streaked, as if the copier was in need of servicing. Still, it was readable. Three large donations had been highlighted with a fluorescent green marker. The donations were at random intervals, yet all were for the same amount—five thousand dollars. It was the name attached to the donations that really piqued the reporter's interest. All three were listed as coming from the generous benevolence of one Bill Murphy of Dogwood Developments.

<hr />

The hallway wasn't crowded at this time in the morning. *Hallway* was probably too dignified a word for the aisle that ran between cubicles at the station house. Some of the junior officers were beginning to show up, undoubtedly trying to get ahead, hoping to impress their superiors. Liu would have liked to impress somebody himself, so he could get out of this mice maze.

One more time, over the phone records. It had bothered him all night. He knew that he recognized the number the break-and-entry guys had called the night of the incident. He just couldn't put his finger on it. He just couldn't remember whose number it was.

He dialed the number slowly, pausing before he punched the very last digit. He'd only have one chance to get a name. Who could it be? Who was most likely? It was time to take a gamble. Maybe this would be his lucky day. Except that Conrad Liu didn't believe much in luck.

"Hello," said a sleepy voice.

Liu paused. Indecision.

"Hello," said the voice a second time, impatiently.

"Hello, Mrs. Andrews?" The detective took a stab.

"Yes," the voice said.

Bingo.

"This is ABC Carpet Shine. We'd like to save you money on your carpet cleaning this year. Would you . . . ?"

"Not interested," the councilman's wife interrupted. "And make sure you take our number off your list, especially if you're going to call this time of the morning," she snapped. "It's supposed to be unlisted."

Thank you, Mrs. Andrews. Conrad Liu smiled as he replaced the phone in the cradle. So Andrews had sponsored the break-in, Liu said to himself. Reckless of him actually. Yet guilt can have a nasty effect on a man, even a powerful man like Philip Andrews.

Mayor Sims was an easy target, for sure, with all his public bluster about progress and urban development—too easy, for the detective's liking. Yes, Sims didn't have any real motive for the crime, which was why Liu had believed the break-in to be routine. Andrews, however, was another story. He had heard the rumors about the councilman—quiet whispers suggesting he was dirty, that his voting pattern contradicted his public image, that he was selling his vote. Liu hadn't paid much attention to any of that until now. It was the telephone number that did it for him. Liu, like many detectives, had a good head for details. He knew he had seen those numbers before, on his Caller I. D. two days before when Andrews had called to point his finger at the mayor.

Of course, Liu reminded himself, he still didn't have a case. It was only a phone call, which would be enough to raise suspicion, but would not be enough to convict. The two young men he had in custody weren't talking. They probably didn't even know who they had been working for. He needed more evidence. He needed some leverage.

―⸺⸻⸻⸺―

Henry was back at the church early. He found it hard to stay away. You can't let go of a life's work all at once. You have to do it in stages. Besides, where was it written that a guy should retire from ministry?

He finished straightening the chairs and setting up the tables. He didn't have to do it, but he knew that it was appreciated. The Leadership Training Team would be meeting tomorrow. Ted had a family and would have enough to do organizing the meeting. Henry didn't think the LTT leader should have to show up any earlier on a Saturday morning than was necessary. His next task was the coffeepot. People would be in and out of the church throughout the day. It was nice if they could have a cup of joe when they arrived.

"So this is what retirement looks like," Jack Newman called out as he entered the fellowship room. Henry jumped slightly. He hadn't heard Jack come in. "I had this picture of palm trees and sandy beaches. . . ."

"Sorry to burst your bubble," Henry said. "Chair stacking and coffee making. That's all the retirement you've got to look forward to."

Jack laughed easily. He knew that Henry and his wife were off to Maui in a few weeks. Besides, if he could have half the peace of mind and purpose when he retired that Henry seemed to have, he'd consider he'd lived successfully.

"So I notice it's Friday," Henry said. "How's that sermon coming along?"

"All done," Jack declared, sounding confident.

"This early in the week?" Henry raised his eyebrows. "You've still got two full days plus a couple of hours Sunday morning before you have to stand and deliver. What are you going to do with all that time?"

"I don't know," Jack admitted. "It's a new experience for me. Maybe I'll actually have to go out and find some people to spend some time with."

"What? The postmodern pastor doing visitation?" Henry laughed.

"Just like the old days," Jack said. "But tell me again, Henry, how did you do it? Is the pastor expected to knock on the door, or is he allowed just to walk right into the house like part of the family?"

"Things really have changed, haven't they," Henry shook his head as he sat down. "But seriously, Jack. You were discouraged about this sermon a few days ago. I was starting to think you might seriously be considering resigning, and now, here you say you're done early? Sounds like a miracle!"

"It's not up there with the parting of the Red Sea," Jack smiled.

"Maybe not, but I'm relieved to hear you've had a good week in the Word of God, and I'm anxious to hear the result on Sunday morning."

"You're awfully gracious to me." Jack looked warmly on the old man. He really loved him. It was such an encouragement to know that Henry was in his corner. He'd heard the horror stories about former pastors. Some never died and never left. They just stayed to curse the incumbent pastor without reprieve until he left or lost his passion for ministry. Henry was everything the stereotype wasn't. Jack enjoyed the man.

"It might be a bit forward of me to suggest it, but I know what I'd do if I had a couple of extra days before I had to preach my sermon," Henry ventured. He was enjoying the attention. It wasn't often that a younger preacher would be this attentive to him.

Right now, Jack felt that he would willingly accept any advice that Henry had to offer. "What would you do, then?"

"Well, believe it or not, I was a young preacher once, and I had a mentor in those days. 'Course, we didn't know the word back then. He was just a man I admired who had good advice for me from time to time."

"Sounds like what you're doing for me," Jack said.

"Maybe so," Henry replied. "Maybe you're my way of giving back the blessing that old guy gave to me all those years ago."

"What did he tell you?" Jack asked. "What was the wisdom?"

"His name was Frank Masters—Reverend Masters we all called him. Even me. I wouldn't think of calling him Frank. I was so much younger than he was, it was impossible for me to think of him as a colleague in ministry. But I tried to get as near to him as I could so I could soak up as much of his wisdom as possible. There was a lot of it to be sponged."

"Appears to me you got yourself pretty well saturated," Jack observed. "You're one of the wise—"

"You're starting to lay it on a little thick, don't you think?" Henry chuckled. "Just listen to what I'm telling you."

Masters was very spiritual. He believed in the classic disciplines. He was like the old-time preachers, spending hours in prayer seeking

God for his people. In all my years in ministry, I don't think I was ever able to live up to the example he offered me."

"Yeah, but you . . ."

"Nonsense." Henry interrupted. "There's no need to butter me up," he said. "I know who I am, and I know, better than anyone, the quality of my former ministry." He shifted in his chair and looked thoughtfully at the ceiling for a few moments. "I remember one time," he continued. "I went to him after my first couple of months in ministry. I had a fairly high estimation of myself and my future. I went to speak to him more out of my own arrogance, looking back on it, than out of any real desire to learn or be guided by the man. However, the question was sound, even if the motivation wasn't. 'Reverend Masters,' I asked the great man, 'how do you get yourself ready to preach?'"

---

*Unless he first hears the message for his own life, he will be ill-prepared to proclaim it to others. . . . He is the proclaimer of God's Word, but he is first a hearer!*

WAYNE V. MCDILL, *THE MOMENT OF TRUTH*, 11

It *was* a good question, Jack thought. It's one thing to have a message from God. It's another to have a sermon constructed that will allow you to communicate that message. But it's yet another thing altogether to be so captivated by the message that you're truly prepared to preach with depth and passion. How *does* one get ready to preach the Word of the living God to distracted and disinclined people?

"I remember him saying to me, 'You know, son, I've always thought that proclamation is a spiritual discipline.'"

"'You mean like prayer, fasting, and meditation?' I asked him."

"'Something like that,' he answered me. He told me that he'd added a whole stage to his preparation for preaching after he'd completed the actual construction of the sermon. I forget what he called it exactly, but I've come to call it *assimilation*," Henry said.

"Reverend Masters thought of it in terms of three elements. The first was *Spirit*. The second was *Word*. The third was *Life*."

"Spirit, Word, and Life," Jack repeated respectfully as he fished for a piece of paper to write it all down.

"*Spirit*," Henry said, "has to do with prayer and power. 'The Spirit's work requires the Spirit's power,' the man said. He reminded me that preaching is about eternal objectives. The old guy was convinced that there was no way possible that he could, by his own strength and eloquence, achieve much of anything that would amount to anything in the final accounting—except it be done by the Spirit."

"Amen," Jack said.

"You say 'Amen,'" Henry observed, "but how many of us get into the pulpit overconfident in the power of our own words? How often have we entered the task feeling a little too good about the way we've put our words together, certain that we're going to knock them dead with that winner illustration?"

"Not too often lately, in my case," Jack lamented.

"And that's why we're having this conversation," Henry said. "We've learned that we're weak, and we want to find the strength that comes in weakness. Masters believed in the power of prayer. He really believed that preaching was the Spirit's work and that, without the unction of the Spirit, he would never have anything life-changing to offer."

"Unction?

### Stage Three: Assimilation

—Unction—
Being filled with the message by the Spirit of God.

"It's an old-timer's word," Henry laughed. "But it oughtn't to be. You should read some E. M. Bounds sometime. Unction is the Spirit's anointing that gives the sermon its power. Without the unction of the Spirit, making the kind of impact that brings about a difference in eternity is just a wish. People don't come into the kingdom without the Spirit leading them."

━━━━━━━

*What the Church needs today is not more machinery or better, not new organizations or more and novel methods, but men whom the Holy Ghost can use—men of prayer, men mighty in prayer.*

E. M. BOUNDS, *POWER THROUGH PRAYER*, 12.

"So, why do we work so hard on our preaching, then," Jack asked, even though he already knew the answer. It was the divine/human oxymoron.

"We do our best, and God does his. Sometimes, he does what he does despite our weakness and our sin."

"But it's no excuse for us easing up or holding back."

"Right," Henry agreed. "For whatever reason in the mystery of God's own mind, the Bible says that God works as his people pray."

"If I want to see a response to my preaching, I need to be personally filled with and empowered by the Spirit, and the only way that will happen is through prayer."

"Much prayer," Henry emphasized. "E. M. Bounds tells the story of an old Scottish preacher by the name of John Welch. The guy thought his day was poorly spent if he didn't spend eight hours of it in prayer, if you can imagine that."

"I can't," Jack admitted.

"He kept a blanket on the floor by his bed, so he could wrap himself up when he rose in the middle of the night to pray. His wife would complain when she found him lying on the ground weeping. He'd say to her, "O woman, I have the souls of three thousand to answer for, and I know not how it is with many of them."

Neither of the men spoke for a moment. Sure, it was an old story and maybe even a little hard to credit. Yet, Jack felt somehow that these old-time preachers knew something that he'd forgotten—if he'd ever known it at all. There's not much point in preaching if you're not prepared to pray.

A door slammed in the distance. It sounded like someone was in the sanctuary upstairs. Hopefully, it's the janitor, Jack thought. Maybe everybody on the church payroll would be early with their work this week.

"So assimilation is about *Spirit*," Jack said, checking his notes. "What about *Word*?"

---

*In Bern, Switzerland, in 1667, church authorities instituted the Bern Preacher Act, which required of preachers that they give their sermons extemporaneously. It stipulated that they must not read the same in front of congregation from notes on paper, which is a mockery to have to watch and which takes away all fruit and grace from the preacher in the eyes of the listeners.*

WAYNE V. MCDILL, *THE MOMENT OF TRUTH*, 137.

"By *Word*, I recall he was talking about the verbalizing of the message. A lot of those guys used to preach extemporaneously—without notes. He'd often write out his sermon in full, but then he'd set it aside and go for long walks in the fields and along the beaches, preaching to himself, to the cows, to the seagulls . . ."

"Like St. Francis of Assisi preaching to the birds," Jack said.

"Something like that," Henry said. "He wanted to get comfortable with the language of the message, so that he wouldn't be overly dependent on a script. He just wanted to be able to look people in the eye and offer them the truth."

"So he would memorize his sermon?" Jack asked.

"Not memorize, so much," Henry answered. "Perhaps there were key sentences and phrases, the first and last few lines of each section maybe, that he'd commit to memory so he could easily keep things moving. But, mostly, it was about mastering the flow of language so that he could comfortably express himself without stumbling over his words."

"You know, hip-hop singers talk about flow," Jack said thoughtfully.

---

*Literates are usually surprised to learn that the bard plan-*
*ning to retell the story he has heard only once wants of-*
*ten to wait a day or so after he had heard the story before*
*he himself repeats it. In memorizing a written text, post-*
*poning its recitation generally weakens recall. An oral*
*poet is not working with texts or in a textual framework.*
*He needs time to let the story sink into his own store of*
*themes and formulas, time to "get with" the story.*

WALTER J. ONG, "ORALITY AND LITERACY IN OUR TIMES," 60.

"You mean those kids with the baggy pants?" Henry asked.

"Henry," Jack feigned surprise. "What radio station have you been listening to?" Both men laughed. "I was just thinking that your Reverend Masters may have been a man ahead of his time. With television and media such a dominant influence in our society, a preacher who can offer his message without notes is going to have a much more effective presentation." Jack thought about it for a moment. "I mean, look at the personalities on television. Whether it's Jay Leno on *The Tonight Show* or Stephen Covey on PBS, none of these guys have notes. They have a dialogue with the audience, unscripted—at least that's how it's made to appear."

"I'm thinking that this would be a lot of extra work," Henry cautioned. "You can't just get up on Sunday morning and wing it. Preaching without notes requires a particularly profound level of assimilation. It takes a lot of extra effort beyond the preparation of the sermon manuscript."

"I think you're right, Henry, but it might be worth it. Sometimes, I find my computer keyboard so limiting in the preparation of a sermon. I feel as if it's restricting me and curtailing my creativity. When I'm working on my computer, I tend to be thinking about grammar and punctuation. I've often thought I could do so much better if I just went for a long run down the back roads behind the church or for a long walk. Then I could work it out orally, the way that people really talk. I think it could be effective."

"Could be," Henry said. "I'd probably still feel more comfortable with a few notes in front of me. I'm not sure how well I could think on my feet, but whichever way we go, we're talking about a level of preparation that most preachers don't give a lot of time to."

"Guilty," Jack smiled, his hand raised in admission.

He found himself studying Henry's face. The laughter looked good on him. The deep lines of a man his age, he couldn't call them worry lines, etched character in his face. I wonder if one day I'll be having a conversation like this with some young preacher coming up, he thought. It would be nice.

"Let's not forget the third aspect, *Life.*" Henry interrupted Jack's thoughts. "Reverend Masters was a practical man. He didn't think a sermon was much good if it couldn't be lived, and he always figured it was important to live his sermon out himself before he preached it. If he couldn't live it, he wouldn't preach it."

"I like that," Jack said.

"He was serious about it, too," Henry said. "I remember hearing him preach through the Ten Commandments. When he got to 'Thou shalt not steal,' the man actually went through his house looking for things that he'd borrowed from others. He returned a stack of books to various lenders and a few old garden tools as well. That was his way of trying to obey the text."

"Obedience to your own sermon is important."

---

*Expository preaching is the communication of a biblical concept, derived from and transmitted through a historical, grammatical, and literary study of a passage in its context, which the Holy Spirit first applies to the personality and experience of the preacher, then through him to his hearers.*

HADDON W. ROBINSON, *BIBLICAL PREACHING*, 20.

"It is," Henry agreed. "It's like Haddon Robinson's famous definition of preaching: 'a biblical concept applied by the Holy Spirit, first to the preacher, then through him to the hearers.'"

"It'll help the preacher identify more effectively with his hearers also, I should think," Jack observed.

"Sure. The listeners get the sense that the preacher lives where they live and understands their experience."

"I don't often do that," Jack observed, "at least not deliberately. My personal application of the sermon is so often abstract. I imagine how I might apply the message if ever I was given the opportunity. It could be interesting to look for ways to put sermons into practice *before* preaching them each week."

———

*Expository preachers determine the biblical truths intended for the persons addressed by the text and then identify similarities in our present condition that require the application of precisely the same truths.*

BRYAN CHAPELL, *CHRIST-CENTERED PREACHING*, 71.

"So, are you ready to preach, then?" Henry smiled.

"I thought so," Jack said. "But now I've got to do some 'assimilating!'" The two men laughed the deep laugh of people who understand one another and are comfortable with one another. "You'll have to thank Reverend Masters for me when you see him," Jack said. "You'll probably see him before I will."

"The man's dead," Henry said. "What are you suggesting?"

"Thank you," Jack said, not answering Henry's mock indignation. "Thanks a lot for your encouragement."

⚘

Jack Newman went home for lunch and found the house empty. It seemed to be empty a lot lately. The kids were growing up and developing their own lives. He made himself a sandwich. Cheeze Whiz and sauerkraut. It was a strange combination he'd learned from his grandfather, but when no one was home he could make what he wanted.

He switched on the kitchen television. He'd long since gotten over the surprise of hearing his brother's voice on the air. "New allegations in the Green Valley break-in surfaced today," Tom Newman announced in his smooth baritone. "An unnamed local politician is under police investigation for influence peddling. *Eye-Witness News* has learned that three donations in the amount of five thousand dollars each were made by Dogwood Developments to the said councilman in exchange for votes on contentious environmental issues."

Jack's fingers went limp, allowing his plate to shatter on the floor. He stood motionless for a moment, his mouth open, then moved quickly to the telephone. Where was the cordless anyway? He tossed seat cushions, moved newspapers, and shifted furniture before finding the delinquent phone underneath a dishtowel on the dining room table. He pressed speed dial number nine. Good, he was home. "Sam," the pastor said, a little breathlessly, "this is Jack. Can you tell me the amounts of those three anonymous cash donations the church has received?"

---

Philip Andrews didn't hear the newscast. While it was true that he was usually in his car at this time of day, driving over to one of his two or three favorite lunch spots, he didn't normally listen to the news. Radio newscasters were just stuffed shirts, Councilman Andrews believed, actors reading scripts. He didn't care to listen to them. So, a few minutes before noon he switched the radio to the oldies station just as he did every day. Tom Newman's bombshell went unnoticed.

---

The three of them met at the church. Jack was the only one of the three with a real office, and they thought it would be quieter there.

Tom Newman brought the donation records. Conrad Liu brought the phone records. Pastor Jack Newman brought the church receipts he'd hurriedly picked up from the treasurer after his phone call. Though the implication was obvious, they still needed some kind of proof. It was a tricky thing. Influence peddling was a serious crime, but it was hard to prove. Someone would almost need to catch the perpetrator red-handed to make a conviction stick.

The three men talked earnestly for forty-five minutes as a plan began to form.

---

Bill Murphy was incensed. It was easier to be angry than scared, though fear was probably more appropriate, given the circumstances. He narrowly avoided kicking his dog as he smashed through the doorway into his home office area. He grabbed the phone, put it to his ear, and stood with his finger poised above the telephone keypad, wanting to dial but not sure who to call. Who *could* he appeal to? Was it time to call his lawyer? He didn't want to overreact. He slammed the phone back down in the cradle and began pacing. What kind of risk was he facing? All the political pressure was on Councilman Andrews, but he, Bill Murphy, was the one who had paid the bribes. He wouldn't be able to avoid the spotlight on something like this, would he? This could be enough to kill the whole development project, he realized. It could perhaps even kill Dogwood Developments. The thought sickened him. It was a misguided idea to begin with. Andrews was only one vote. Yet council had been evenly divided on development issues for years. Andrews' single vote had usually been enough to get him the go ahead. Now, with Tom Newman's broadcast revelation, the whole thing could blow up in his face. What should he do? He just didn't know.

---

Jack saw his brother to the front door of the church. The detective had left a few moments earlier. He wandered into the sanctuary and took a seat in one of the pews. He realized he was sitting in Philip

Andrews's accustomed seat—whenever he showed up, that is. The thought surprised him. It was almost creepy. He resisted the urge to get up. Instead, he tried to think what the councillor must have been thinking. It was strange. Jack didn't always understand the mysterious ways of his people. What kind of spiritual guilt would motivate a man, a powerful man, to do such a thing? What must he have been thinking as he listened to me preach? Did I have any impact at all on the man?

Jack stood up and ambled over to the pulpit. He stopped about ten feet away from the ancient desk and examined it as if he'd never seen it before. It wasn't actually as large as it seemed to him from the other side. It *was* old. He wondered who had built it. Stepping up to the pulpit, Jack examined it more closely to see if he could find some indication. Carefully, he searched the various edges and alcoves, nooks and niches. There didn't appear to be any plates, imprints, or stickers with the name of a particular company or craftsman. Perhaps it had been homemade by a member of the church. If so, whoever it was had done a fine job. The joints were exquisite, tightly fitted, and perfectly matched. It must have taken hours, Jack thought. No power tools, everything by hand—the craftsman must have had incredible patience.

The finish was worn. There were rough scratches, some of them in surprising places. There was a deep gouge in the middle of the podium surface. How it got there, Jack could not imagine. The pulpit should be refinished, he thought. A little TLC and furniture polish would do wonders for it. Then again, it would be a shame to remove the evidence of its history. The scratches were like beauty marks, character lines in the face of a grand old lady.

———

*A right spirit from a biblical standpoint is the oxymoronic combination of confidence and humility.*

LEONARD SWEET, *SOULTSUNAMI,* 312

Jack walked back to where he'd been sitting and picked up his file of sermon notes. He returned to the pulpit and laid them all out on the desk. Henry's comments that morning had made an impression on him. Jack had been living this sermon all week, but it wasn't until now that he realized how directly the message of his text reflected the experience of his life. How do you explain the mysterious ways of people? How do you know the truth about God? In a world where everything appears to be contingent and subject to the moment, how can you confidently stand and speak truth as from the mouth of God? Where does a person find the necessary humility? How can a person preach?

The pulpit helps, of course. It's the physical representation of spiritual and ecclesiastical authority, but in the end how was it anything more than one person's craftsmanship. It was not Mt. Sinai, the place of divine pronouncement. Nor was it Aaron's calf, a crafted substitute for the worship of the divine. It was what it was—a place where preachers, irrepressibly weak and unfortunately flawed, could stand and speak, by the grace of God, the truth of God. The mystery is solved in Christ who indwells, making God known to us. Christ in me, the hope of glory. He said it out loud, very loud. "Christ in me, the hope of glory." He whispered it softly. "Christ in me, the hope of glory."

Jack fell to his knees and prayed. It was a seminal prayer—a watershed prayer. Magnificent. The words, the ideas, the passions, came gushing out of the deepest places in his soul like seawater exploiting a hole in a dike. Long hidden and repressed, his puny spirit swelled and triumphed. He imagined that moment long ago when the hand of God tore the veil into pieces, and he saw with his heart's eye, he felt with his soul's passion, the presence of God in his life. For the first time in a very long time, Jack Newman *believed* he could preach.

───────

Stephen Lang was locking up late for a Friday night. It had been a long week, and he was only now feeling like the Green Valley Trust office was getting back into order. His car was parked on the curb just outside the office door. He noticed Jack Newman coming down the sidewalk. Obviously, the pastor had been working late as well. He was going to shout a greeting, but then caught himself. Newman walked right by him without so much as a hello, muttering something unintelligible, as if he were trying on words for size.

I hope his Sunday sermon is more coherent, Lang shrugged as he climbed into his Hyundai.

# 6

# Fourth Stage: Delivery
## THE EVENT

Jack swung his arm in the direction of the alarm clock, sending his Bible, two books, his wristwatch, and a half-empty glass of water crashing to the floor. The clock remained unscathed, emitting the shrillest, most obnoxious beeping sound that the manufacturers could invent. It served its purpose. Pastor Newman was awake now. The clock showed five-thirty in the morning.

He did not normally rise this early. He wasn't even sure that he could previously have attested that such a time of day existed. Yet, it was no mistake. The kids hadn't been fiddling with the alarm mechanism. He'd set it early himself so he could spend extra time in prayer. Jack anticipated a special morning, not only because of the extra-curricular events that would transpire at church later on, although overcoming all of that would require special prayer in and of itself, but also because of the amazing week he'd spent in preparation. He was beginning to understand his listeners and he'd taken steps to prepare a message that just might make a difference this time. At least, it would be a step in the right direction. Perhaps this Sunday morning would be a turning point for him in his ministry. That arrogant pulpit might never get the best of him again.

Philip Andrews was up early in the morning as well, yet for him it was more habit than anything. He liked to start his morning before anyone else in the house had risen. A cup of coffee, the newspaper, and a quiet house helped him get his head into a place where he could deal reasonably with the demands of public life.

He slipped on his worn, leather slippers, grabbed his white, terry robe, and made his way downstairs in the dark. Opening the front door, he noticed the sun just starting to make its appearance, a tinge of orange growing over the eastern horizon. The days were getting longer. Summer would bring a nice reprieve from all this, he thought. He picked up the newspaper and glanced quickly at the front page. He was always relieved when he didn't find his own face staring back at him. Funny how that goes. There'd been a time when he would grab the paper eagerly, scouring it for anything personal, looking for the publicity that was essential to a politician's career. Now, it was just the opposite. A no-news day was a good day.

He picked up his coffee on the way back to his study and nestled into the comfortable easy chair that was his accustomed spot for reading the paper. He set the coffee down and unfolded the broadsheet. A fat envelope fell into his lap. Instinctively, Andrews pushed it down between his legs and looked up nervously to see if anyone had noticed. It was silly, of course; no one was ever up this time of the morning. His heart pumping hard, he allowed himself to take the envelope in his hand, testing it for weight. It felt about the same thickness as the others.

Andrews felt ill. This thing was out of control. He hadn't expected a payment—no, an *envelope*, at this point. As far as he knew, there were no appropriate votes coming up for his attention. He'd intended to call a halt to the whole thing. The arrangement sickened him, but he'd never been able to get up the courage to confront Bill Murphy directly on the issue. How do you stop something that was never really started in the first place?

He'd met Murphy at a reception, one of those harmless free lunches sponsored by Dogwood Developments. They'd had a friendly chat, nothing more. Andrews may have let on that he wasn't as "green" as his press clippings had indicated. He may have let slip that he was a "pragmatic politician" with an open mind and a willingness to consider "fresh ideas" about the future of the city.

It wasn't long after that when the first envelope had arrived, lying innocently in his desktop inbox, thick with cash. No note. No identifying marks of any kind. Yet, Andrews knew where it came from, and he knew exactly what was expected of him. He'd played along, surprising his colleagues on council with his apparent about-face. But he told them, and he told himself, that he was voting his conscience, and that development proposal was in the best interest of the community.

And yet there was the speech. At first Andrews thought that he had to back up his vote with a consistent public face, so he had stood up at a campaign dinner and had delivered a sound critique of the environmental movement, Green Valley Trust in particular. Bill Murphy had been pleased, but the reaction from Andrews's constituency had been harsh. Newspaper coverage had stirred up a lot of unwanted trouble for him. Shrewdly, Andrews realized that he didn't need to change his rhetoric to match his voting record. People didn't pay very close attention when it came right down to it, and so his speeches had been "green" ever since. Murphy didn't seem to mind as long as the votes kept coming through. The next time a Dogwood Development proposal came before council, Andrews voted for the developer and the money followed.

Andrews was worried. It had never really been about the money. He was really only interested in the political support a powerful man like Bill Murphy could provide. The money, quite frankly, had terrified him. He'd leave this envelope unopened just as he had done the previous three times. Putting the money in the church offering plate was a way of easing his conscience. He'd even gone so far as officially disclosing the donations. No one ever looked at disclosure statements, but if pressure was at some point brought to bear, Andrews wanted to make sure that Murphy was tied in with him. The declaration would make the money look less like what it was—a bribe.

With every envelope, his sense of guilt had increased. He'd occasionally see Bill Murphy at public events or in a crowd. The money was never acknowledged; nothing ever said. To speak of it would feel like an admission of guilt. Andrews was actually starting to talk himself into believing in his new voting pattern. After all, he'd never actually profited from the money.

Of course, the break-in revealed his guilty conscience. He was far beyond any sense of principle, and he well knew it. He had heard the rumors. Who knows how long people had been whispering about his misdeeds. If even *he* had heard them, the stories must have made the rounds. Strange how little stock he *used* to put in gossip.

He had panicked, of course. One of the rumors held that Green Valley had a file on him, that they had been gathering information to use against him. That irritated the councilman, leading him to act irrationally. He got into his car with a wallet full of cash. He drove and kept driving until the street in his rearview mirror grew narrow and the lights grew dim. He found two young men idling on a street corner, offered them money, and gave them his phone number. "Call me when it's done," he had said.

Philip Andrews stood up from his chair and looked out the window. There was a van he didn't recognize parked in front of his house, its windows darkly tinted. Sighing deeply, he moved back toward the kitchen. Good thing it's Sunday, he told himself, as he tucked the money into the pocket of his robe.

—⚒—

Tom Newman had not been to church in a very long time. He often felt guilty about it, though not because he felt any sense of religious responsibility. His feelings had more to do with a sense of obligation to his brother. He knew how hard Jack worked and how sincere he was about his calling. But, of course, that wasn't the only reason Tom was brushing his teeth so early on a Sunday. He put the toothbrush back in the cabinet and walked over to his clothes closet. He ran his hand across his row of journalist suits. Wardrobe obviously wouldn't be a problem.

Tom chose a sober-looking dark blue, the kind of suit he would wear to a formal dinner or perhaps to the funeral of an acquaintance. It might, in fact, be somebody's funeral at church this morning, Tom chuckled to himself.

---

Conrad Liu woke up to his cell phone.

"He's got the package," the voice said a little too energetically for this time of the morning, the detective thought.

"Were you able to see what he did with it?"

"Sure. We had a clear view into his study through the window. He didn't do a thing with it—just seemed a little embarrassed when he found it. It looked like he was trying to hide it under the newspaper while he checked it out. This guy's strange."

"People tend to act strangely when they're about to do something stupid." Liu signed off and set the phone on the table by the bed. He stretched a little and rubbed his eyes. *I shouldn't have to get up this early on a Sunday,* he thought to himself. *The sacrifices I have to make for this job! Can't remember when I was last in church.*

---

The Reverend Jackson Newman, M.Div., stood at the back of the church and listened briefly to the organist. Amazing how she kept her concentration with all the noise and carrying on. He decided that people used to come into worship more respectfully. They used to sit quietly, preparing themselves silently to meet with God. Now, people took the opportunity to say hello to friends and catch up on the week's news. It made for a good sense of community, but it didn't add much to a sense of reverence.

Jack breathed deeply and began his walk into the sanctuary, the unwritten signal that worship was about to begin. Chin up, back straight, head high. He could still hear his father's voice in the back of his mind, "Walk proud, son. Stand up straight and command respect." Somehow, the advice seemed less significant this morning. All of the effort he'd always put toward dressing correctly, gesturing correctly, and speaking correctly had its place, but he wasn't concentrating on those things this morning. He was focused on his mission.

———

*To preach the Gospel is not just to tell the truth but to tell
the truth in love, and to tell the truth in love means to tell
it with concern not only for the truth that is being told but
with concern also for the people it is being told to.*

FREDERICK BUECHNER, *TELLING THE TRUTH*, 8.

The pastor took his seat on the platform near the pulpit, not because he had to, but because he liked to. He enjoyed watching people
worship. Scanning the crowd before preaching helped him to sense
what was at stake in the event. As their pastor, he knew things about
people in the congregation, like the woman in the fourth row on the
left side, sitting by herself. Her husband wasn't with her. She had been
telling people that he was out of town on business, but Jack knew the
truth. The young man slouching down in the second from the last
row in the middle section was doing his best to look disinterested. It
wasn't cool to show too much interest in church. Yet, Jack had talked
to him just two weeks ago. The boy had admitted some of his deeper
feelings to the pastor. Jack knew that there was more going on in this
young man than met the eye. The couple in the second row had lost
their child last year. The man in the front had just received an unex-
pected promotion. The man handing out programs in the back was
worried about an upcoming doctor's visit. Jack looked at them all, and
he loved them. His pastor's heart was in good working order.

It was a larger crowd than usual, and the singing seemed spirited.
Jack thought he could detect a genuine enthusiasm for the service that
morning. On the other hand, it could have been just his own optimism.
It had been a long time since he'd looked forward to his sermon with
such anticipation.

Of course, the crowd size was enhanced by the presence of Police
Detective Conrad Liu, looking like a stereotype in his rumpled rain-
coat and too-dark suit. All he needed was the sunglasses. Liu had found
the furthest possible seat from the pulpit, back in the corner in the
little half-row beside the sound booth. It was a good spot for him, ac-

tually. He wouldn't be noticed there, but he'd be able to see every-thing that was going on.

Jack's brother Tom was also in attendance, looking impeccable as always. Jack had a hard time taking his gaze off his brother once he'd spotted him. He knew that Tom had come for professional reasons, yet still it warmed his heart to see him in the congregation. No mat-ter what it was that had got Tom there, the thing was, he was there. Jack would preach the Word, and he was confident that God could use it to speak even into the deep places of this journalist's jaded heart.

Of course, there were others—a couple of uniformed police officers, hidden away in Jack's office. When the time came, they'd be available.

Sam Sidhu was not in his normal seat in the second row. The trea-surer had been tipped-off, and the excitement was too much for him. Jack could see him pacing impatiently in the foyer of the church.

Most importantly, Philip Andrews was sitting in his newly accus-tomed spot, looking uneasy, but trying not to. There had been an un-comfortable moment prior to the service when Andrews had bumped into Tom Newman on the way in, but Tom had acted like a pro, jok-ing that it was about time he came to hear his brother preach. Andrews appeared convinced, though he probably would have preferred to avoid his media nemesis. Tom knew enough to sit well away from the coun-cilman. Not so far, Jack noticed, that he wouldn't be able to see what was going on as the service continued with yet another repetition of "Lord, I Lift Your Name on High."

Jack turned his attention to the old pulpit. It didn't look anywhere near so intimidating from the back. So much microphone cord spilled out of it that the preacher always had to be careful not to trip. There were two shelves inside the pulpit, both of which were littered with old church bulletins. Anyone wanting to write the history of this church would have to look no farther, Jack thought with a grin. Some of those bulletins were probably almost prehistoric. Then, there was a series of small holes drilled in its bottom panel. Years ago, someone had the ill-considered idea of installing a speaker there. The speaker was long gone, but the holes would be there forever. The carpet was worn where the preacher stood. Obviously, I don't move around too much, Jack realized.

Jack thought about how interesting it was that something so ordinary and so human could be the place of so much power. Amazing things had happened over the years as preachers had opened God's Word standing behind this very piece of furniture. Could something special happen here today?

——◦◦◦◦◦——

The ushers rose to take the offering. Liu threw a few dollars in the plate as it passed by. Jack wondered if he'd be adding the amount to his expense account. Tom Newman appeared to be writing a check. His brother had always been generous to him. But of course, four set of eyes were on Philip Andrews as he pulled a very fat envelope out of his breast pocket and set it in the plate, trying his best to be discreet.

Conrad Liu rose immediately and made to leave as if retiring to the washroom. Tom Newman gave him a knowing nod as the detective passed him in the aisle. Sam Sidhu, looking very excited, collected the plates from the ushers and led the detective into the pastor's study.

The pastor himself, from his privileged viewpoint, was able to see the whole thing. But, of course, now it was time to put all of that out of his mind. Now, it was time to preach.

━━━━━━━━━

*. . . some men are made for manuscripts, and some for the open platform. . . .*

PHILLIPS BROOKS, *ON PREACHING*, 170.

Jack stepped boldly up to the pulpit. He paused for a moment before setting aside his notes. He'd assimilated the sermon so well that he wouldn't need them. He simply announced his text, Colossians 1:24–29, and read it with conviction. Many said later they could not remember when their pastor had shown such energy and passion. It was not that he was ranting. The pulpit would not feel his fist. Instead, he spoke with a conversational passion that was at once inviting and arresting.

"To them God has chosen to make known among the Gentiles the glorious riches of this mystery, which is Christ in you, the hope of glory."

━━━━━━━

*Either way, if ever I lose my fear of preaching and my frustration at my own inadequacies in that task, I suspect it will be a sign that I ought to quit.*

IAN PITT-WATSON, *A PRIMER FOR PREACHERS*, 16.

Jack led the congregation in prayer. It was a simple prayer. Jack asked that God would speak, that the Divine himself would be the preacher here this morning. Jack asked, as sincerely as he knew how, that God would make truth known by his Spirit in the preaching of this sermon in this place.

He paused as he looked up from his prayer. It was a longer pause than the people were used to. Gradually, several of them looked up, curiously, as if to ask whether or not the preacher was planning on saying anything that particular morning. Jack was afraid, but it was a different kind of fear. For once, he was not afraid of the people, whether they would like his presentation, whether or not he would have to fend off the angry advances of disenchanted deacons in the hallway after the service. This time his fear was more nobly channeled. The fear Jack felt this morning was the fear of God, and it motivated him. There was so much at stake. As Spurgeon once said, "Life, death, hell, and worlds unknown hang on the preaching and the hearing of a sermon." He paused. He prayed silently. And then, he spoke.

---

*To hear this sermon as it was originally preached at Parkland Fellowship, Surrey, B.C., in August of 2000, log onto www.preaching.org.*

"Life is full of mystery!" He said it confidently. He said it with force. He said it as if the whole congregation knew it to be true. "I live much of my life in a constant state of bewilderment and befuddlement," Jack continued. "There are so many things I experience in this world on a daily basis that I don't know the first thing about. Like the telephone. Two years ago I took a trip to Israel to see the Holy Land. I picked up the telephone and called the office here to see if everything was all right. The call came through in seconds. Pastor Henry picked it up, and I immediately knew it was him just from the sound of his voice. I could tell how he was feeling and what kind of a day he was having, not so much because of what he said, but because of the way he said it. Do you remember, Henry?"

"I remember," the elder pastor said warmly.

"I could hear the nuances of Henry's voice from the other side of the planet! It's amazing! How can this be? How is this possible? It's a mystery!" Jack was getting worked up.

"Does anybody here know how the television works? How about the microwave? I don't understand gravity. I don't understand government." Philip Andrews stirred a little bit on that one. "I certainly don't understand women. I don't understand the engine in my car—and don't even get me started on computers." Jack said this with a smile on his face. Laughter washed over the congregation as people began to identify with the spirit of Jack's presentation. "It's a mystery!"

"But there are bigger mysteries than this in life." Jack's voice suggested he was getting serious. "How do I know what love is? Can I ever know the truth for certain? And maybe the biggest one of all: How do I understand God?"

"There are only two ways you can go with mystery," Jack suggested. "You can eliminate it, or you can embrace it. If you want to eliminate it, you call a detective. You bring in someone who can sort out all the clues, line up all the facts, and make sense of them all. The way you eliminate a mystery is to solve it—to take the mystery out of life. On the other hand, you could celebrate mystery! Enjoy the ambiguities and take pleasure in the paradox. Who needs to solve a mystery, when you can embrace it." Jack spoke expansively and aggressively. People noticed a fresh sense of urgency in his voice.

"'The truth is out there,' they say on the television program *The X-Files*. Scully is always trying to eliminate mysteries while Mulder is always embracing them. The tension between the two characters is what made the show so popular. The truth is out there—or is it?"

"What do we know, and how do we know it? What do we believe, and why do we believe it? Can we really know anything for sure? What about God? It was a problem for Paul preaching in Colossae." Jack was trying to make the transition to the text as seamless as possible, integrating the undergirding story of the text with the listener's story, helping his listeners to connect with Paul's listeners. "If you lived in Colossae, what were you going to believe? Which way were you going to go? You had a lot of options. There were a lot of ways to think about God and truth and the bigger questions in life. The Jews had their ideas, and the Greeks had their ideas, and in between there were the philosophers and the cultists, the Gnostics and the mystics. Then, there was Paul talking about Jesus. You could go any direction you wanted. You could believe anything that you could think of. Build your own god. The whole enterprise was ambiguous. Find your own path and make it work the best way that you could. Life was, indeed life *is* full of mystery."

Jack took a long pause to catch his breath. He was about to make the transition into the second quadrant. His purpose had been to engage the listeners with the story of the text. It wasn't a narrative text, so there wasn't a lot of story to work with, but by the look on the faces of his listeners it appeared that he'd been able to get the people involved. There was a hush in the congregation, a sense of expectation that Jack hadn't noticed in a very long time. Time to start teaching, Jack told himself.

"Jesus solves the mystery." Put bluntly like that, the point had a slightly jarring effect on the congregation. "Life is full of mystery, but Jesus came to solve the mystery. Jesus came to make truth known to us. Jesus came to make God known to us."

Change of pace, Jack reminded himself. The people are engaged.
I've got them listening. Now I've got to help them understand the point
of the text. Jack began by illustrating the point. "I love Agatha Christie
stories, don't you? Miss Marple, wheedling out the truth in her grand-
motherly way. Hercule Poirot and his 'little gray cells.' They're not
too complicated, as stories go. Somebody dies early on, and there are
always five or six people who could be responsible. The detective
spends his or her time assembling and organizing the various facts
and clues that may or may not be pertinent to the solution and then,
after about forty-five minutes or 150 pages, whichever the case might
be, the main characters are all assembled in the parlor for the final
scene. There the detective lays out the information, makes the truth
known to them, and reveals the murderer.

"It may be a bit of a stretch," Jack continued, "and I mean no dis-
respect, but could we see Jesus as our Poirot? How about Jesus as our
detective—the one who lays out the facts and makes sense of them
all for us. Jesus, our detective, revealing truth to us and making *God*
known to us. It's the parlor scene, the final days, and Jesus is solving
the mystery for us."

More explanation, Jack told himself. "Under the old covenant, God
had been the proprietary interest of the Jewish people. God belonged
to the Jews, and he was known and served by priestly practices behind closed doors and heavy curtains. 'Trust me,' the priests said, and
the people did. Either that or turn to one of the local cults or philosophies. It was all very mysterious.

"But do you remember what happened when Jesus went to the
cross? The Bible says that the veil that kept the priest hidden from
the people was ripped in two from the top to the bottom, as if by the
hand of God himself. The secrets were laid bare, the truth was made
available, and it was all because of Jesus. This mystery," Jack went to
the text, "that had been kept hidden for ages and generations, verse
26, was now being made known, was now being disclosed to the saints.

"You can know the truth." Jack was *preaching* now. "You can know
God. Why? Because of Jesus who is 'Christ in you,' revealing God to
you, indwelling you—the hope of glory." Jack said it again, "He is your
hope of glory."

"The first chapter of Colossians makes the point that all the fullness of the godhead dwells bodily in Jesus Christ, and here, by the time we get to the end of the chapter, we are told that all that fullness, all that God is in Christ, dwells in *us*. All the fullness of God is in Christ, and all the fullness of Christ is in us when we put our faith in him. Christ is in us, making it possible for us to know God, to appreciate God. The mystery is less mysterious. Jesus, our great detective, solves the mystery."

In the pastor's study, Conrad Liu, Sam Sidhu, and the two police officers opened a familiar-looking, plain white envelope stuffed with cash and matched the serial numbers to those on a list Liu produced from his pocket. Videotape from a camera hidden in the sanctuary was being checked to confirm the envelope had come from the hand of Philip Andrews.

Liu looked up from his task. Seems awfully quiet up there, he said to himself. I wonder how it's going.

"But what's wrong with a little mystery?" Jack asked, after an appropriately long pause. He was moving into the third quadrant now, doing battle with the listeners' innate cognitive objections. So far, things had gone well, but he had not done much yet to convince the listeners, at least not at the deep level necessary to help them *want* to reckon with the text. The message was fine as far as it went, but at this point it was just the preacher's convictions on the table. It was time to go for commitment on the part of the listeners, to grapple with their own sense of authority. In order to do that, he'd have to speak with the listeners' voices. He'd have to speak for them, anticipating their objections and treating those objections faithfully.

"It's too simplistic, isn't it?" Jack asked. "It's a nice, neat answer to a very complicated question. It's the Sunday school answer to everything. Every child in third grade knows that the way to get straight

A's in Sunday school is to answer 'Jesus' to every question that comes along. It can't possibly be that simple, can it?"

Tom Newman leaned forward on his seat. Jack had just described his thought process exactly. His interest level was deepening.

"It's a big old world out there," Jack admitted. "It's complicated and uncertain. The further we send our telescopes into outer space, the more mystery we find. The sharper we can focus our microscopes, the more questions we discover."

It seems to me I've heard this before, Tom smiled to himself, recalling their lunchtime conversation over Chinese food.

"Quantum mechanics, Heisenberg's uncertainty principle, the Hubble telescope—the more precise our instruments of observation and understanding, the more we find that paradox is fundamental. There is mystery in the most elemental aspects of human life.

"So, how could we know anything for sure," Jack continued. "Isn't it a little dishonest, intellectually, to load the whole thing onto Jesus' plate? Wouldn't it be better for us just to welcome the mystery and accept the ambiguity? Shouldn't we just accept the reality that life is too wild and too weird and let go of our need to make sense of it all? What would be wrong with that? What's wrong with a little mystery? Maybe we should all move back to Colossae where we can make our own choices and build our own gods and do what we like. Maybe we already have."

Tom knew that this was no homiletical ploy. Jack was sincerely struggling with the implications of his point. He found his journalistic cynicism had been voided by Jack's honest presentation.

"I'm actually describing a very old problem. It's the problem of the object and the subject. How can people, locked in time and space, describe or understand what transcends time and space? How can a sinner know the holy? How can the finite grasp the infinite?"

Jack waited dramatically. The questions hung suspended like museum pieces. Tom found himself wanting to reach out and take hold of them, but he wasn't sure how to find the handle. "My answer," Jack was almost whispering, "goes all the way back to Sunday school. My answer is Jesus.

"You can know the truth, because God reveals it to you." Time to close the case, Jack told himself. Be convincing. "It's not that you're so intelligent. It's not that you've somehow found the secret that allows you personally to transcend the limits of this mortal plain. You can know the truth, because God tells you the truth, because God is in the business of revealing the truth. He does it through Jesus."

Henry was smiling widely. Turns out Jack had been listening carefully on Tuesday morning. Henry was surprised at the way he felt himself responding to this preacher's honest passion.

———<br>

"The real mystery is that Jesus loves us," Jack reminded them. "Why would God care enough to tell us the truth? Why would he provide so costly an answer? Why would Jesus love us when all we've ever done is to try to concoct ways to avoid him? No, there's plenty of mystery in this deal yet. But as God speaks to us in Jesus, adequately, if not exhaustively, we can know the truth—though we'll never master it."

———<br>

Philip Andrews was starting to feel it. He was a hard-shelled man who came to church just for appearance's sake. This was about politics, not about penitence, yet the message was starting to get to him. He'd never been able to admit how ashamed he was of his actions. The money was bad enough. The break-in was maybe the worst idea he'd ever had. Here he was, sitting in church, while two innocent men sat in jail because of his impulsive attempt to divert attention. The truth was, the mayor was a good man. That he would stoop to try and sully the mayor's good name indicated how far he'd fallen. He had a moral compass, though it hadn't been kept in good working order. He believed in God, though he'd failed to see the relevance of faith. Life had been about finding his own way and discovering his own truth. He'd been making it up as he went along, and he'd been doing a pretty good job of it, at least until the last few months. He'd achieved power and position. Money had never been a problem. Yet here he was, feeling broken and incomplete.

Was it possible that there really was something more than power games? he wondered. Could God actually care about the choices I've made in politics and in my life? Is that why I'm feeling so crummy? Is that why I've acted so poorly? Could I really get to know God through Jesus somehow, like this pastor is talking about? Large cracks were forming in Philip Andrews's well-developed shell.

⟶⠒⠒⠒⠒⟵

Bring it home, Jack said to himself. Time to make this thing *sing!* "Do you remember reading mysteries as a kid? I used to stay up long after dark with a flashlight under the covers. Whodunit? There were always so many possibilities. It could have been the jealous aunt, or the conniving brother, or the suspicious foreigner. Then again, there was always the butler. It's no wonder I couldn't turn the light off, no way I could quit turning pages. I had to know *whodunit.* I had to know what would happen. Mysteries are engaging.

"Whodunit?" Jack looked the congregation in the eye. "Jesus dunit. Jesus done it all. Jesus loved us. Jesus died for us. Jesus dwells within us. Jesus tells truth to us. Jesus shows God to us. He is our hope of glory.

"We can live our life in a fog. We can invent our own convictions. We can live tentatively, uncertainly, indefinitely. We can stumble in the darkness of our own dubious indecision.

"Or we can listen to God. We can engage the mystery and live in the energy of Christ. We can live confidently in the knowledge that God has a purpose for us. We can live in the glory of the hope that is Christ. We can find our future and trust in His promise. We can proclaim truth to a world that desperately needs a hopeful message. We can know God in all of his glorious mystery, and we can know him now."

Jack stopped to catch his breath. A wry twist came across his lips. "Life still baffles me," he confided. "Like, how exactly *do* they get the caramel into the caramilk? Or, why is it that the Chicago Cubs never seem to win? Or," long pause, "why does God love me?" Longer pause. "It's a mystery—a wonderful, glorious mystery."

Jack didn't have anything left to say. He sat down. His heart was pounding. Sweat was dripping from his brow. He wasn't sure what he'd planned to do at this point in the service. He couldn't remember whether they were going to sing another song. Maybe he should lead in prayer. That might be a good thing . . .

Tom Newman wasn't sure what the correct protocol was for a moment such as this. He wanted to stand and applaud, but his instincts told him that wouldn't be appropriate. There was something deeper going on inside of him. He would have to talk to Jack about it over dinner.

Conrad Liu came down the stairs, his uniformed colleagues at the ready. Something unusual seemed to be going on in the sanctuary, though he had no idea what it was. The place was eerily silent. Jack Newman was sitting unceremoniously on the steps beside the pulpit, his eyes closed, his head and shoulders leaning heavily against the wooden side.

The setup had worked perfectly. The money the police had planted in Philip Andrews' newspaper matched exactly what Andrews put into the offering plate. Liu doubted that the councilman had even opened the envelope. They couldn't actually arrest him, of course. There was nothing illegal about giving money to one's church. The evidence of impropriety was all circumstantial. Yet, Andrews was a man with a guilty conscience. Liu was betting that he would come with them quietly. Ten minutes of questioning at police headquarters and he would confess the whole thing. Conrad Liu had great confidence in his powers of inquisition.

Philip Andrews stood, as if on cue, determination hardened in his face. He stood in place without moving for a long, awkward time. Liu took a step forward and gave a nervous look of warning to the uniform on his right.

Something was going on. Jack looked up and saw the politician moving slowly up the aisle. Instinctively, Jack moved to meet him, his arms opening, a smile warming on his face.

Tom Newman found himself rising, though he wasn't sure just why. Perhaps it was in support of this extraordinary meeting. Perhaps he stood to his feet as a first tentative step of his own faith and, in doing so, led others, several of them all over the building, to follow his example.

Andrews had something to say, though it came out garbled. Jack had nothing left to say. The two men embraced, and the angels in heaven celebrated.

---

What happened after that was confusing to just about everyone. As people exited the building, they were stunned to see the councilman escorted away by the police. Henry had tried to intervene, but Jack's brother Tom had steered him away, trying awkwardly to explain. Conrad Liu was baffled by Andrews's peaceful disposition. Andrews, for his part, was quite willing to submit. His lawyer would fight, of course. The whole thing could be denied. His politician's mind could come up with a dozen strategies to avoid conviction. Yet, it didn't matter to him anymore. He had just stood before a much higher court and been declared not guilty. He would confess the whole thing, telling them anything they wanted to know and accepting the consequences of his actions here on earth.

---

Eventually, the clamor died down, and as the last people straggled out, Jack heaved a great sigh. He climbed back up to the pulpit and gripped the two sides tightly in his familiar preacher's stance. He was feeling at home in the old pulpit. This was right. This was good. Jack *was* a preacher—a truth-telling, pro-claiming, preacher. God had spoken this morning, and what postmodern person could dare to argue with that?

He gathered up his notes and stuffed them into the cover of his Bible. Leaving the sanctuary, he stopped for one last look at the arrogant, old pulpit. It had a majestic, mysterious look about it.

Jack turned off the light and exited the building, his mind and his heart active and full. Sunday was only seven days away. He had a sermon to think about.

# Appendix A

# An Integrative Model for Preaching

This is the article Jack Newman read in chapter four of this book. Kenton C. Anderson, "An Integrative Model for Preaching" can be found at www.preaching.org (March 2001).

My daughter and I had a disturbing conversation a few months ago. It was a typical father/daughter discussion. She wanted to do something I thought might be inappropriate and I said so with all the fatherly tenderness and respect I thought necessary for such an occasion. She was quick, however, to sense the nature of my rebuke. "Dad, I don't need to hear a sermon," she said as she turned her back on me and walked away. She was nine years old.

Her response stung, given that I make my living preparing and delivering sermons. Unfortunately, it is not only my daughter who has decided that listening to sermons has become unnecessary. It would appear that the whole culture has concluded that preaching is anachronistic, that it is at best a relic of bygone times and at worst an arrogant abuse of religious authority.

I have concluded, however, that the Lord has not revoked my calling and that he still expects me to preach. Still, it seems to me that preaching in these days might demand some fresh thinking and an alternate form.

## Principles: Theology and Theory

### Authority: "Oh yeah, who says?"

There are two primary issues relevant to the task of preaching. The first relates to the matter of authority. Anyone who wishes to persuade must provide warrant for his or her claim. It may have been in distant times that listeners would attend sermons in an agreeable and docile frame of mind, unquestioningly receiving whatever the preacher cared to suggest. Those listeners have long since been replaced by a newer more skeptical group who listen with one finger on their mental remote control, challenging the preacher to prove that this sermon is worth the investment of their time and energy.

"Love one another," the preacher says, "be good to your enemies."

"Oh yeah," the listener responds, "who says?"

"Well, God says," the preacher answers, and it is a good answer. God created us and holds the creator's right to dictate and decree. Unfortunately, many of those we speak to may not find this to be enough. Listeners today come ready-built with their own authority. They could choose to daydream or close their mind. They could get up and walk noisily out, shaking their fist all the way. The listener has power in the transaction known as preaching and they are not afraid to use it. The preacher, then, must make an authority level choice between text and today, between objectivity and subjectivity, between divine authority and human authority.

| Authority |
|:---:|

Text———————————Today

On the one hand, the case is made on the basis of God's revealed Word. "Thus saith the Lord," settles the question.

On the other hand, the point is established upon the foundation of the listeners' own preset assumptions and experiences. "Sounds about right," the listeners say, processing the message through their inborn authority system.

### Apprehension: "OK. How can I help you?"

The second primary concern for the preacher is to discover the most effective means of helping the listener own the truth. Apprehension is the taking hold of a truth, like a policeman apprehending a suspect or a student taking hold of a book. It is the preacher's desire that the listener take hold of the message being offered.

There are two primary approaches a preacher can choose. The first is by means of explanation, and the second is by means of experience.

**Apprehension**

Explanation——————————————Experience

Traditionally, preachers have emphasized the cognitive path, explaining the propositions of the text and sermon, making things clear and making things orderly. The idea is that if the truth is made comprehensible to the mind, the listener will be compelled to respond, and the preacher will have done his or her job.

More recently, preachers have been rediscovering intuitive experience as an avenue to listener apprehension. Gripping stories and emotional appeal compel a listener to respond to the message on offer. Whether the propositions can be explained is less important when a listener *feels* a need to respond.

### Integration: "Refuse to choose."

The recent history of homiletics has tended to describe a spasmodic lurching from pole to pole in the struggle between text and today, explanation and experience. Cognitive forms of exposition square off against more intuitive narrative sermon forms. Text-based authority structures stand against listener-based "seeker" forms or preaching. In the end, however, such polarized approaches might not be helpful.

Integration describes the bringing together of seemingly contrary options in such a way that the integrity of each substance remains uncompromised. Is it possible that preachers could integrate text and today, explanation and experience? Is it possible that preachers could refuse to choose?

Overlaying the two continuums, authority and apprehension, creates an interesting opportunity for preachers to integrate these seemingly opposing concerns.

Move 1: experience (apprehension) of the text (authority)
Move 2: explanation (apprehension) of the text (authority)
Move 3: explanation (apprehension) of today (authority)
Move 4: experience (apprehension) of today (authority)

God endorsed integration as a means of communication in the incarnation of his son, Jesus Christ. The Word becoming flesh is more than just an analogy of the preaching task. It is the substance of the preacher's message.

## Process: Discovery, Construction, Assimilation, and Delivery

### First Stage: Discovery (The Message)

The first stage in the preparation of a sermon, then, is *discovery.* Specifically, the preacher seeks to discover the *message,* which is "what God wants to say through this text to these people at this time." It is an unrepeatable, virtually unpublishable moment in time when the people encounter the voice of God through the Word of God for their unique moment and place in history. The message can be discerned by four simple questions corresponding to the above four integrative moves.

Move 1: What's the story?
Move 2: What's the point?
Move 3: What's the problem?
Move 4: What's the difference?

1.  What's the story (experience of the text)? Even in the book of Hebrews, there is always a story. There really were Hebrew

people with a story. Identifying that story can help the listener
see the humanity in the text, creating an experiential encounter with the message that will not easily be shaken off.

2. What's the point (explanation of the text)? The Bible, while not
   exclusively propositional, is conceptual in its makeup. The
   Bible offers truth that can be examined, detailed, ordered, and,
   for the most part, understood. The preacher need not shy away
   from offering points, well explained and carefully put.

3. What's the problem (explanation of today)? The problem with
   biblical propositions is that they are not so easily accepted. The
   Bible is profoundly counter-cultural. If a preacher offers biblical truth with honesty and integrity, there will be inherent
   conflict in the engagement with contemporary listener presuppositions. Acknowledging the problem from the perspective of
   the thinking human will be important if we care about listener
   comprehension and assent.

4. What's the difference (experience of today)? Of course, head
   knowledge without heart response is hardly worth the effort.
   Every text intends a difference in the life response of listeners
   as they grow in obedience to the God who created them.

Answering these four questions will lead the preacher to know what
it is that God is saying to these people through this text at this time.

### Second Stage: Construction (The Sermon)

The second stage in homiletic presentation is construction. What
is to be constructed is the sermon, which is simply a structure sufficient to communicate the message. Just because a preacher has an
understanding of the message does not mean that he or she is ready
to preach. The preacher needs a sermon, a vehicle that will help the
people hear from God.

The preacher is wise to begin by seeking to get the listeners involved
(engaged) in the message. It is no longer wise to assume that the listeners will invest the energy needed to engage themselves in the experience. Having gained the listeners' involvement in the process, the
preacher can declare the propositions offered by the text (teaching).

From there, the preacher ought to work to convince the listeners of the truth of the teaching. Finally, the preacher needs to motivate the listeners to think about the implications of the message. The preacher is looking to encourage a response.

The concepts chosen by the preacher need to have appropriate language and argumentation in order to address the following important listener issues:

Move 1: "So what?"         (Tell the story.)
Move 2: "What's what?"     (Make the point.)
Move 3: "Yeah, but . . ."  (Engage the problem.)
Move 4: "Now what?"        (Imagine the difference.)

1.  In the first move, the preacher seeks to convince the listeners of the relevance of the message. The listeners need to be given a reason to listen. Usually, this is most effectively achieved by getting the listeners emotionally involved, connecting their own stories with that of the biblical text.
2.  In the second move, the preacher makes the point overt. This is the place for explanation—only so much explanation as is necessary to inform the listeners' minds without bogging them down with confusing details. The challenge is to be clear and intellectually stimulating.
3.  In the third move, the preacher acknowledges the listeners' objections, seeking to overcome the inevitable reticence the listeners will harbor. Minds don't change without a fight. Preachers who can get under the surface and deal with the real cognitive objections of the listeners will speak powerfully.
4.  In the fourth move, the preacher offers the possibility of a tangible, alternate future according to the call of the gospel. Biblical texts intend substantive life change. Our sermons must intend no less.

### Stage Three: Assimilation (Unction)

Many preachers, having discovered their message and constructed their sermon, understand their task to have been completed. But there is another stage that is essential to powerful, biblical preaching. This is the stage in which the preacher seeks the "unction" of the Holy

Spirit, the empowering passion that makes a sermon live. The preacher must be filled with the message from God by the Spirit of God.

Assimilation involves three concerns, *spirit*, *word*, and *life*.

### Assimilation: Spirit, Word, Life

*Spirit* refers to the *power* of the Holy Spirit that gives the sermon its impact. Preaching intends eternal impact for spiritual purposes. Spiritual business cannot be accomplished without the Spirit's power. This kind of power is only accessed through prayer—a great deal of fervent *prayer*. While it is important that the preacher bathe the entire process of preparation in dedicated prayer, it is helpful at this stage in the process to engage in a protracted time of intentional prayer. One is not prepared to preach until one has truly met with God.

*Word* refers to the practical business of choosing and assembling the language of the sermon. Whether the preacher chooses to sit down at a computer and write the sermon or rather to go on long walks to consider how to say what needs to be said, the preacher needs time for *working it out*. Wrestling with the language of the sermon is an important use of time and energy at this point in the process. The preacher needs to struggle at *locking it in*, striving not so much to memorize the words, but to grow comfortable with the language, perhaps committing key phrases and transition points to memory.

The process of assimilation is an attempt to embed the sermon in the mind and character of the preacher prior to preaching. To that end, the concept of *life* is most crucial. The preacher ought to look intentionally toward ways to obey the message of the sermon. *Obedience* to the claims of the text on the part of the preacher is important to win the approval of the listeners. Further, the effective preacher will pursue *identification* with the lives and experiences of the listeners. The congregation needs to sense that the preacher understands their lives and that the sermon is more than theoretical.

### Stage Four: Delivery (The Event)

The sermon event is a unique moment in time when people hear from God. Virtually unpublishable, the sermon is much more than just the words that are uttered. It is a dynamic event in which people are able to hear from God by means of the preacher. An inviting physical style coupled with conversational passion and a minimum of obstacles (including even pulpits and notes) will enhance the possibility that the listeners will be drawn into the presence of the Lord.

Preachers shouldn't get too stressed about manipulating the physical aspects, gestures, and appearances of the preaching event. For instance, to wear a tie or not to wear a tie is not a moral question but a pragmatic question. If the tie will impede our presentation (as it probably would on Friday night with a group of teenagers), then we should not wear it. If not wearing a tie will be an impediment, then we had better put it on. The preacher ought to embrace whatever helps the listener hear from God.

One of the mysteries of preaching is that God would use a human instrument at all. Human preachers are tempted to get in the way of the task, fearing people (which leads to debilitation) instead of fearing God (which offers motivation). Yet God, for his own good reasons, has chosen to integrate the human with the divine in the process of making his Word known. God uses preachers!

A few years ago while attending a conference on preaching in Boston, I returned to my hotel room late in the evening and turned on the television. Much to my delight, they were broadcasting a hockey game between the Boston Bruins and my beloved Vancouver Canucks. I confess, however, that I spent most of the time thinking more about preaching than hockey. I noticed, as the team was returning to the ice from the dressing room for the second period, a motivational saying that was embedded in the carpet in the hallway out toward the ice. This was the last thing the players saw before stepping out onto the playing surface, and it struck me that, while it was good advice for hockey players, it was even better advice for preachers. It said, "Master technique, but let the Spirit prevail."

We do the best we are capable of to master the various theories and techniques of the homiletical task, but in the end the power belongs to the Spirit of God. We do our part, but if anything of eternal importance and value is going to happen in the sermon event it will be his doing.

---

*Master technique, but let the Spirit prevail!*

# Appendix B

# Integrative Preaching: A Summary

## Theoretical Principles:

| | | |
|---|---|---|
| Authority ("Oh yeah? Who says?"): | text | today |
| Apprehension ("OK. How can I help you?): | explanation | experience |

## Stage One: Discovery

Message: What is God saying through this text to these people at this time?

| | |
|---|---|
| Move 1: What's the story? | Experience and Text |
| Move 2: What's the point? | Explanation and Text |
| Move 3: What's the problem? | Explanation and Today |
| Move 4: What's the difference? | Experience and Today |

## Stage Two: Construction

Sermon: A framework capable of communicating the Message.
1. So what?          (Tell the story.)
2. What's what?       (Make the point.)
3. Yeah, but . . .    (Engage the problem.)
4. Now what?         (Imagine the difference.)

## Stage Three: Assimilation

Unction: Being filled with the message from God by the power of God.
   Spirit:            prayer              power
   Word:             working it out       locking it in
   Life:              obedience           identification

## Stage Four: Delivery

Event: The unique moment in time when people hear from God.
   Fear:             fear of man          fear of God
   Manuscript:        written (full/partial)  oral
   Physical Style:     whatever helps       conversational passion

# Works Cited

Anderson, Kenton C. "'Global' Preaching: A Paradigm for Preaching Across Cultural Change." Ph.D. diss., Southwestern Baptist Theological Seminary, 1997.

Bakhtin, Mikhail. "Marxism and the Philosophy of Language." In *The Rhetorical Tradition: Readings from Classical Times to the Present*, edited by Patricia Bizzell and Bruce Herzberg, and translated by Ladislaw Matejka and I. R. Titunik. Boston: Bedford Books of St. Martin's Press, 1990.

Barth, Karl. *Homiletics*. Translated by Geoffrey W. Bromiley and Donald E. Daniels. Louisville: Westminster/John Knox, 1991.

Bartow, Charles L. *God's Human Speech: A Practical Theology of Proclamation*. Grand Rapids: Eerdmans, 1997.

Brooks, Phillips. *On Preaching*. New York: Seabury, 1964.

Bounds, E. M. *Power Through Prayer*. Grand Rapids: Zondervan, 1962.

Buechner, Frederick. *Telling the Truth: The Gospel as Tragedy, Comedy, and Fairy Tale*. San Francisco: Harper & Row, 1977.

Capon, Robert Farrar. *The Foolishness of Preaching: Proclaiming the Gospel Against the Wisdom of the World*. Grand Rapids: Eerdmans, 1998.

Chapell, Bryan. *Christ-Centered Preaching: Redeeming the Expository Sermon*. Grand Rapids: Baker, 1994.

Collins, James C., and Jerry I. Porras. *Built to Last: Successful Habits of Visionary Companies*. New York: HarperBusiness, 1994.

Craddock, Fred. *Preaching*. Nashville: Abingdon, 1985.

Dostoyevsky, Fyodor. *Crime and Punishment.* Translated by David McDuff. London: Penguin, 1991.

Fant, Clyde E. *Preaching for Today.* 2d ed. San Francisco: Harper & Row, 1987.

Fulford, Robert. *The Triumph of Narrative: Storytelling in the Age of Mass Culture.* Toronto: House of Anansi Press, 1999.

Grenz, Stanley J. *A Primer on Postmodernism.* Grand Rapids: Eerdmans, 1996.

———. "Star Trek and the Next Generation: Postmodernism and the Future of Evangelical Theology." In *The Challenge of Postmodernism: An Evangelical Engagement,* edited by David S. Dockery, 89–103. Wheaton, Ill.: Victor, 1995.

Lowry, Eugene L. *Doing Time in the Pulpit: The Relationship Between Narrative and Preaching.* Nashville: Abingdon, 1985.

Madison, G. B. *The Hermeneutics of Postmodernity: Figures and Themes.* Bloomington, Ind.: University of Indiana Press, 1988.

Mayhue, Richard L. "Rediscovering Expository Preaching." In *Rediscovering Expository Preaching: Balancing the Science and Art of Biblical Exposition,* by John MacArthur Jr. and the Master's Seminary Faculty. Edited by Richard L. Mayhue and Robert L. Thomas, 3–21. Dallas: Word, 1990.

McDill, Wayne V. *The Moment of Truth: A Guide to Effective Sermon Delivery.* Nashville: Broadman & Holman, 1999.

Meyers, Robin R. *With Ears to Hear: Preaching as Self-Persuasion.* Cleveland: Pilgrim, 1993.

Middleton, J. Richard, and Brian J. Walsh. *Truth Is Stranger Than It Used to Be.* Downers Grove, Ill.: InterVarsity, 1995.

Miller, Calvin. *Marketplace Preaching: How to Return the Sermon to Where it Belongs.* Grand Rapids: Baker, 1957.

———. *The Empowered Communicator.* Nashville: Broadman & Holman, 1994.

Ong, Walter J. "Orality and Literacy in Our Times." *Journal of Communication* 30 (winter 1980): 197–204.

Piper, John. *The Supremacy of God in Preaching.* Grand Rapids: Baker, 1990.

Pitt-Watson, Ian. *A Primer for Preachers.* Grand Rapids: Baker, 1986.

Placher, William C. *The Domestication of Transcendence: How Modern Thinking About God Went Wrong.* Louisville: Westminster/John Knox, 1996.

Robinson, Haddon W. *Biblical Preaching: The Development and Delivery of Expository Sermons.* Grand Rapids: Baker, 1980.

Seuss, Dr. *On Beyond Zebra.* New York: Random House, 1980.

Stafford, T. P. "Expository Preaching: A Criticism." *The Review and Expositor* 8 (April 1911): 225–33.

Stott, John R. W. *Between Two Worlds: The Art of Preaching in the Twentieth Century.* Grand Rapids: Eerdmans, 1982.

Sweet, Leonard. *SoulTsunami: Sink or Swim in the New Millennium Culture.* Grand Rapids: Zondervan, 1999.

Thiselton, Anthony C. *The Two Horizons: New Testament Hermeneutics and Philo-sophical Description with Special Reference to Heidegger, Bultmann, Gadamer, and Wittgenstein.* Grand Rapids: Eerdmans, 1980.

Vanhoozer, Kevin J. *Is There a Meaning in This Text? The Bible, the Reader, and the Morality of Literary Knowledge.* Grand Rapids: Zondervan, 1998.

Webb, Joseph M. "Pluralism and the Search for a 'New Gospel.'" Papers of the An-nual Meeting, 32d ed., 56–65. Oakland, Calif.: Academy of Homiletics, 1997.

Willhite, Keith. "Audience Relevance and Rhetorical Argumentation in Expository Preaching: A Historical-Critical Comparative Analysis of Selected Sermons of John F. MacArthur Jr. and Charles R. Swindoll, 1970–1990." Ph.D. diss., Purdue University, 1990.

Willimon, William H. *Peculiar Speech: Preaching to the Baptized.* Grand Rapids: Eerdmans, 1992.

# Works Consulted

Allen, Diogenes. *Christian Belief in a Postmodern World: The Full Wealth of Conviction.* Louisville: Westminster/John Knox, 1989.

Allen, Ronald J., Barbara Shires Blaisdell, and Scott Black Johnstone. *Theology for Preaching: Authority, Truth and Knowledge of God in a Postmodern Ethos.* Nashville: Abingdon, 1997.

Anderson, Raymond E. "Kierkegaard's Theory of Communication." *Speech Monographs* 30 (March 1963): 1–15.

Anderson, Walter Truett. *Reality Isn't What it Used to Be: Theatrical Politics, Ready-to-Wear Religion, Global Myths, Primitive Chic, and Other Wonders of the Postmodern World.* San Francisco: Harper & Row, 1990.

Aristotle. "Rhetoric." In *The Rhetorical Tradition: Readings from Classical Times to the Present,* edited by Patricia Bizzell and Bruce Herzberg, 151–94. Translated by W. Rhys Roberts. Boston: Bedford Books of St. Martin's Press, 1990.

Augustine. "On Christian Doctrine, Book IV." In *The Rhetorical Tradition: Readings from Classical Times to the Present,* edited by Patricia Bizzell and Bruce Herzberg, 386–422. Translated by Therese Sullivan. Boston: Bedford Books of St. Martin's Press, 1990.

Babin, Pierre, and Mercedes Iannone. *The New Era in Religious Communication.* Translated by David Smith. Minneapolis: Fortress, 1991.

Broadus, John Albert. *On the Preparation and Delivery of Sermons.* 4th ed. Revised by Vernon L. Stanfield. San Francisco: Harper Collins, 1979.

Brooks, Phillips. *Lectures on Preaching: Delivered before the Divinity School of Yale College in January and February, 1877.* New York: E. P. Dutton, 1877.

Brown, H. C., Jr., Gordon Clinard, and Jesse Northcutt. *Steps to the Sermon: A Plan for Sermon Preparation.* Nashville: Broadman, 1963.

Brueggemann, Walter. *Finally Comes the Poet: Daring Speech for Proclamation.* Minneapolis: Fortress, 1989.

———. *Texts Under Negotiation: The Bible and Postmodern Imagination.* Minneapolis: Fortress, 1993.

Brunner, Emil. *The Divine-Human Encounter.* Philadelphia: Westminster, 1943.

Buttrick, David. *A Captive Voice: The Liberation of Preaching.* Louisville: Westminster/John Knox, 1994.

———. *Homiletic: Moves and Structures.* Philadelphia: Fortress, 1987.

Caputo, John D. *Radical Hermeneutics: Repetition, Deconstruction and the Hermeneutic Project.* Bloomington, Ind.: Indiana University Press, 1987.

———. "When Narrative Is Not Enough." Unpublished paper presented to the Academy of Homiletics in Atlanta, December 2, 1995.

Connor, Steven. *Postmodernist Culture: An Introduction to Theories of the Contemporary.* Oxford: Basil Blackwell, 1989.

Craddock, Fred B. *As One Without Authority.* 3d ed. Nashville: Abingdon, 1979.

Davis, Henry Grady. *Design for Preaching.* Philadelphia: Fortress, 1958.

Erickson, Millard J. *Evangelical Interpretation: Perspectives on Hermeneutical Issues.* Grand Rapids: Baker, 1993.

———. "Revelation." In *Foundations for Biblical Interpretation: A Complete Library of Tools and Resources,* edited by David S. Dockery, Kenneth A. Matthews, and Robert B. Sloan, 3–18. Nashville: Broadman & Holman, 1994.

Erickson, Millard J., and James L. Heflin. *Old Wine in New Wineskins: Doctrinal Preaching in a Changing World.* Grand Rapids: Baker, 1997.

Eslinger, Richard L., ed. *A New Hearing: Living Options in Homiletic Method.* Nashville: Abingdon, 1987.

———. *Intersections: Post-Critical Studies in Preaching.* Grand Rapids: Eerdmans, 1994.

———. *Pitfalls in Preaching.* Grand Rapids: Eerdmans, 1996.

Fant, Clyde E. *Preaching for Today.* 2d ed. San Francisco: Harper & Row, 1987.

Fosdick, Harry Emerson. "What Is the Matter with Preaching?" *College of the Bible Quarterly* 29 (October 1952): 5–18.

Galli, Mark, and Craig Brian Larson. *Preaching That Connects: Using the Techniques of Journalists to Add Interest to Your Sermons.* Grand Rapids: Baker, 1994.

Glodo, Michael J. "The Bible in Stereo: New Opportunities for Biblical Interpretation in an A-Rational Age." In *The Challenge of Postmodernism: An Evangelical Engagement,* edited by David S. Dockery, 148–72. Wheaton, Ill.: Victor Books, 1995.

Greidanus, Sidney. *The Modern Preacher and the Ancient Text: Interpreting and Preaching Biblical Literature.* Grand Rapids: Eerdmans, 1988.

Harvey, David. *The Condition of Postmodernity: An Enquiry into the Origins of Cultural Change.* Oxford: Basil Blackwell, 1989.

Henry, Carl F. H. "Postmodernism: The New Spectre?" In *The Challenge of Postmodernism: An Evangelical Engagement*, edited by David S. Dockery, 34–52. Wheaton, Ill.: Victor Books, 1995.

Hull, William E. "The Contemporary World and the Preaching Task." In *Handbook of Contemporary Preaching*, edited by Michael Duduit, 571–87. Nashville: Broadman, 1992.

Hybels, Bill, Stuart Briscoe, and Haddon Robinson. *Mastering Contemporary Preaching*. Portland: Multnomah, 1989.

Jensen, Richard A. *Telling the Story: Variety and Imagination in Preaching*. Minneapolis: Augsburg, 1980.

Johnson, Mark Alan. "Christological Preaching for the Postmodern Era." Ph.D. diss., The Southern Baptist Theological Seminary, 1994.

Kenneson, Philip D. "There's No Such Thing as Objective Truth, and It's a Good Thing, Too." In *Christian Apologetics in the Postmodern World*, edited by Timothy R. Phillips and Dennis L. Okholm, 155–70. Downers Grove, Ill.: InterVarsity, 1995.

Koller, Charles W. *Expository Preaching Without Notes*. Grand Rapids: Baker, 1962.

Lischer, Richard. *A Theology of Preaching: The Dynamics of the Gospel*. 2d ed. Durham: Labyrinth, 1992.

———. "The Limits of Story." *Interpretation* 38 (January 1984): 26–38.

———. *Theories of Preaching: Selected Readings in the Homiletical Tradition*. Durham: Labyrinth, 1987.

Long, Thomas G. *Preaching and the Literary Forms of the Bible*. Philadelphia: Fortress, 1989.

———. *The Witness of Preaching*. Louisville: Westminster/John Knox, 1989.

———. *The Homiletic Plot: The Sermon as Narrative Art Form*. Atlanta: John Knox, 1980.

Lundin, Roger. "The Pragmatics of Postmodernity." In *Christian Apologetics in the Postmodern World*, edited by Timothy R. Phillips and Dennis L. Okholm, 24–38. Downers Grove, Ill.: InterVarsity, 1995.

———. *The Culture of Interpretation: Christian Faith and the Postmodern World*. Grand Rapids: Eerdmans, 1993.

MacArthur, John, Jr., and the Master's Seminary Faculty. *Rediscovering Expository Preaching: Balancing the Science and Art of Biblical Exposition*. Edited by Richard L. Mayhue and Robert L. Thomas. Dallas: Word, 1990.

MacNeil, Robert. "Is Television Shortening Our Attention Span?" *New York University Education Quarterly* 14 (winter 1983): 2–5.

Mawhinney, Bruce. *Preaching with Freshness*. Grand Rapids: Kregel, 1997.

McGrath, Alistair. "The Christian's Response to Pluralism." *Journal of the Evangelical Theological Society* 35 (December 1992): 487–501.

McLuhan, Marshall. *Understanding Media: The Extensions of Man*. With an introduction by Lewis H. Lapham. Cambridge: MIT, 1994.

———. *The Medium and the Light: Reflections on Religion.* Edited by Eric McLuhan and Jacek Szklarek. Toronto: Stoddart, 1999.

Meyers, Robin R. *With Ears to Hear: Preaching as Self-Persuasion.* Cleveland: Pilgrim, 1993.

Middleton, J. Richard, and Brian J. Walsh. *The Transforming Vision: Shaping a Christian World View.* Downers Grove, Ill.: InterVarsity, 1995.

———. *Truth Is Stranger Than It Used to Be.* Downers Grove, Ill.: InterVarsity, 1995.

Mounce, Robert H. *The Essential Nature of New Testament Preaching.* Grand Rapids: Eerdmans, 1960.

Oden, Thomas C. *After Modernity . . . What?: Agenda for Theology.* Grand Rapids: Academie, 1990.

———. *Orality and Literacy: The Technologizing of the Word.* New York: Routledge, 1982.

Phillips, Timothy R., and Dennis Okholm, eds. *Christian Apologetics in the Postmodern World.* Downers Grove, Ill.: InterVarsity, 1995.

Postman, Neil. *Amusing Ourselves to Death: Public Discourse in the Age of Show Business.* New York: Penguin, 1985.

Randolph, David James. *The Renewal of Preaching.* Philadelphia: Fortress, 1969.

Reid, Robert Stephen. "Postmodernism and the Function of the New Homiletic in Post-Christendom Congregations." *Homiletic* 20 (winter 1995): 1–13.

Reid, Robert, David Fleer, and Jeffrey Bullock. "Preaching as the Creation of an Experience: The Not-So-Rational Revolution of the New Homiletic." *The Journal of Communication and Religion* 18 (March 1995): 1–9.

Ricoeur, Paul. *Interpretation Theory: Discourse and the Surplus of Meaning.* Fort Worth: Texas Christian University Press, 1976.

Rorty, Richard. *Contingency, Irony, and Solidarity.* Cambridge: Cambridge University Press, 1989.

Steege, Mark J. "Can Expository Preaching Still Be Relevant in These Days?" *The Springfielder* 34 (March 1971): 261–66.

Steimle, Edmund A., Morris J. Niedenthal, and Charles L. Rice, eds. *Preaching the Story.* Philadelphia: Fortress, 1980.

Sunukjian, Donald Robert. "The Homiletical Theory of Expository Preaching." Ph.D. diss., University of California, Los Angeles, 1974.

Veith, Gene Edward, Jr. *Postmodern Times: A Christian Guide to Contemporary Thought and Culture.* Turning Point Christian Worldview Series. Edited by Marvin Olasky. Wheaton, Ill.: Crossway, 1994.

Wells, David. *God in the Wasteland: The Reality of Truth in a World of Fading Dreams.* Grand Rapids: Eerdmans, 1994.

Wilson, Paul Scott. *The Practice of Preaching.* Nashville: Abingdon, 1995.

Wingren, Gustaf. *The Living Word: A Theological Study of Preaching and the Church.* Philadelphia: Fortress, 1960.